Freiburg: From class tramway to light rai

Ray Deacon

Published by
Light Rail Transit Association
PO Box 302
Gloucester GL4 4ZD
ISBN 0 948106 22 0

Contents

Bertoldsbrunnen, the heart of the city of Freiburg. The elegant Martinstor predominates in this peaceful Sunday view of GT4 car 112 passing Bertold's fountain, as it turns into Kaiser-Joseph-Strasse on route to Zähringen. Note the absence of motor vehicles and the Bächle flowing gently through the street.

(author)

A perfect study of the Schwabentor, circa 1952, with maximum-traction motor car 52 heading east on route 3. The narrow street to the of the tower is now part of the ring-road and many of the houses were demolished to make way for a car park. (K.

Foreword

Local Traffic in Freiburg - A Success Story

Freiburg im Breisgau is known for its very sunny location, outstanding wine and the beauty of the city, which has retained its medieval buildings. The scenery and culture are the basis of an incomparable quality of life.

The desire to maintain this standard of life and continue with improvements to the environment, led to the recognition by the politicians of the environmental lobby's priority on public transport.

The backbone of this system is the *Stadtbahn* which reaches two-thirds of the population and transports them to the heart of the city at Bertoldsbrunnen. Here, pedestrians and public transport present a picture of co-operation where each complements the other. A high service frequency that does not require a timetable, unimpeded travel outside the inner city on segregated tracks operated with low-entrance vehicles, a simple and attractive fare structure and development of a travel region covering 3 000 square kilometres, presents a system that nearly all the 200 000 inhabitants claim to use once a day.

The quality of the technical development of the transport system, in conjunction with the fare structure and marketing, have more than doubled the number of passengers in 10 years, from under 30 million to 66 million per year. For the successful implementation of its local traffic plan, Freiburg received the first European Traffic Award in February 1996.

With this, the Freiburg traffic system has reached a definitive conclusion. A further increase in the number of passengers, and a shift in travel patterns in favour of public transport, is only possible if route capacity is increased. The development of the *Stadtbahn* is also a prerequisite for the development of the region if the city is to meet the quality standards required.

Under the title *Breisgau-S-Bahn 2005*, the infrastructure, vehicles and frequency of use should build towards an integrated system for the Breisgau region. These measures are forecast to increase the number of passengers by 30%.

Successful local traffic politics is a continuing experience........

Prof. Dr. Rolf-Michael Kretschmer.
Chairman, Freiburger Verkehrs AG

ar 121 is currently the only GT4 car to see regular operation in Freiburg, following its conversion to a party car in 1995. It is seen here queezing" through the narrow archway under the former police station, in to the pretty Kloster Platz in Günterstal, 7/93   (author)

Introduction

Development of Freiburg

The attractive city of Freiburg Im Breisgau is situated in the *Land* (state) of Baden-Württemberg in the south-west corner of Germany, 20 kilometres east of the river Rhine and the border with the Alsace region of France. It has a population of 200 000 and is often referred to as the gateway to the Black Forest. It is a popular tourist and conference centre and has a flourishing trade in timber, wine, textiles, chemicals and musical instruments.

Freiburg first came to prominence in 1120 when the Dukes of Zähringen, the brothers Bertold III and Konrad, founded a settlement below a *Schloss* (castle). Ideally located on the old Black Forest trade route between Swabia and Alsace; the population of 200 steadily grew and had reached 9000 by 1320. It was the combination of the rich deposits of silver and its favourable position on the trade route, that gave Freiburg its dominant status.

As the centuries passed, the city succumbed to a succession of foreign rulers, from the Austrians, Swedes, Bavarians and French, to the House of Baden in 1806. During the *Thirty Years' War* (1618-48), Freiburg and the surrounding area were the sites of several major battles between the French and Austrian-Bavarian armies.

Freiburg gradually evolved into a thriving cultural centre, with a University dating from 1457, the State Academy of Music, the State Training School for Sculptors and Stonemasons, a teachers training college and five technical colleges. The *Rote Bären* (Red Bear) inn, which dates from 1311 and is believed to be the oldest inn in Germany, is located in Oberlinden.

The city's most prominent feature however is the 120-metre-high spire of the *Münster*. One of the finest Gothic ecclesiastical structures in Germany, its construction began in the 13th century and took four centuries to complete.

The opening of the Karlsruhe to Basel railway 1845, signalled the beginning of a boom in housing construction which gradually encompassed the villages of Herdern, Stühlinger, Haslach and Lorettoberg. The city was built around two main arterial roads on north-south and east-west axes, with their crossing point at Bertoldsbrunnen. Later construction projects were concentrated mainly on the western fringes of the city.

The city escaped the physical destruction of the first world war, and in 1919 an elected National Assembly drew up a new constitution for *Land Baden*, which incorporated Freiburg. Later, in 1935, Baden became an administrative unit of the *Third Reich*.

Heavy allied bombing destroyed a large part of the central area in 1944, but much of its charm was recreated in the subsequent rebuilding. In 1947, Freiburg became the seat for a newly formed *Land* of Baden, a position it retained until 1952 when it was incorporated within an enlarged *Land* of Baden-Württemberg.

Life in Freiburg is easy-going, making it a favourite retreat for young and old. Summertime can be extremely hot, but the streets are often cooled by a breeze blowing down from the *Höllental* (Hell Valley). Little streams called *Bächle* trickle gently through open gulleys in the cobbled streets and, like many towns and cities in Germany, the central area is prohibited to private vehicular traffic. A broad selection of museums and a full programme of plays, operas and concerts provide a wide range of entertainment.

Early public transport services were started in the 1890s by an entrepreneur using horse-drawn covered wagons in the streets. Electric trams took over in 1901, and by the early 'thirties the system had grown to its prewar maximum. Following a period of uncertainty and contraction in the 1960s, the decision was taken to modernise and extend the tramway. Subsequent developments have seen the construction of segregated routes operating to *Stadtbahn* standards using fast, high-capacity tramcars, supported by a network of urban bus routes. Many of these suffice as feeders to the tramway and will either contract or disappear as the tramway expands. As the number of people using public transport continues to rise and more motorists are enticed from their cars, the citizens of Freiburg can look forward to a safer, cleaner and congestion free environment.

I have been a regular visitor to the Black Forest for the past 25 years and have studied the developments on Freiburg's tramway since its recovery from near closure in the early 1970s. My intention when writing this book was to produce an historical record of the tramway, from its modest beginning to the well patronised *Stadtbahn* system of the present day. A detailed outline of plans for its continued expansion completes the picture.

Acknowledgements

It would not have been possible to produce this book without the invaluable help and assistance of several people. In particular, I would like to offer my sincere and grateful thanks to:

The staff of the **Freiburger Verkehrs AG**, for providing documentation and information on the current operation of the tramway and proposals for its future expansion.

Andreas and **Lukas Kaufhold** (FFSeV), for access to and the loan of historical photographs from their extensive collection, and factual verification of the text.

Jack Wyse (LRTA), for advice and guidance on the textual content, for proof reading the draft text and assistance with designing the fleet list tables.

Roger Smith, for producing an excellent series of maps.

Janet Taplin, (Just My Type) for typesetting the draft text and the final design of the page layout.

To all others whose names are accredited with having taken specific photographs.

Not least to my wife Rosemary and son Kees for their patience and understanding every time I dashed off to take that one last shot.

Ray Deacon, Blackboys, Sussex. April 1998.

1. From horse bus to electric tram

Horse buses

Most electric tramways in Germany were converted from horse-drawn routes, but this was not the case in Freiburg where public transport began with privately-owned horse-drawn "carts" operating limited bus services, mainly for the benefit of the working population.

Growing demand for a regular service encouraged one of the "cart" owners, Josef Amann, to introduce a scheduled service in the summer of 1891, using horse-drawn "carts" fitted with canvas top covers. The route ran between the city boundaries near Siegesdenkmal and Lorettostrasse, along the main north-south road. A few services continued south to the village of Günterstal, a total distance of 5.2 km (1 mile = 1.6 km).

Amann's operation was so successful that he opened two more routes in the autumn of 1891. The first was a short working between Albertstrasse and Schillerstrasse, and the second linked the main railway station or *Hauptbahnhof* (Hbf) with Nägeleseestrasse on the east-west road.

By the summer of 1894 the services were operating on a 15-minute headway on all three routes, with the exception of the section from Lorettostrasse to Günterstal which ran every 30 minutes. Increasing debts, however, forced Amann to apply for a subsidy from the City Council, but when this was rejected, he closed his operation down.

A boisterous public response ensured that public transport remained at the top of the Council agenda, but deliberations took forever in 19th century Freiburg. Eventually, the Council provided finance for Adolf Jenne, a local riding school owner, to run a service on the Siegesdenkmal – Lorettostrasse route. Jenne purchased seven so-called *Tramwagen*, conventional horse tram bodies mounted on cart-type wheels, from Basel, and started operating on 31 October 1896.

On 1 October 1897, he reopened the Hauptbahnhof – Nägeleseestrasse route and a new route running from the city through Günterstal to Kyburg. Each route was identified by a roman numeral:

I **Siegesdenkmal** – Bertoldsbrunnen – Kaiserstrasse – **Lorettostrasse**

II **Hbf** – Bertoldsbrunnen – Salzstrasse – Schwabentor – **Nägeleseestrasse**

III **Freiburg** – Günterstal – **Kyburg**

These two photographs from the horse-bus era, show "Tramwagen" 5 (ex-Basel 10) approaching the Kaiserbrücke on route for the city (below), while "Tramwagen" 2 (ex-Basel 7), heads north along Kaiserstrasse towards Siegesdenkmal (left), circa 1898.
(collection Kaufhold/Hettinger)

3

A fare of 20 *Pfennige* (Pf) was charged on route 1, and 15 Pf on route II. Passengers travelling south of Lorettostrasse had to pay an additional 2 Pf.

The Council, meanwhile, had published a proposal for a conventional horse tram system, followed shortly after by another for an electric tramway, but public opposition to overhead wires curtailed further progress.

A *Commission fur die Strassenbahn* was formed under the direction of Josef Amann and a Councillor Tafel, with a brief to carry out a study of transport systems in other parts of Germany. Its report, dated 9 July 1897, stressed that most towns in Germany were electrifying their horse tramways, and that a horse-drawn system in Freiburg would be obsolete by the time it opened. It concluded that an electric tramway was the only viable solution.

Plans for electric trams

On 8 May 1899, the Council announced its intention to introduce electric trams, on routes extending to the villages of Littenweiler, Haslach, St Georgen, Betzenhausen, Herdern and Zähringen.

Meanwhile another *Commission* was formed to select the best method of supplying electricity to the city. An experienced electrical engineer, Emil Eitner, who had just finished installing a power generating system in Kassel, was engaged as Manager of the electricity undertaking in Freiburg. He was also given the task of constructing and managing the city's tramway and on 10 May 1900, he awarded Siemens & Halske of Berlin a contract for the construction of a metre-gauge system operating four routes:

A: Rennweg – Siegesdenkmal – Bertoldsbrunnen – **Lorettostrasse**.

(A 2.7-km, double-track short-working of route **D**)

B: Hbf – Bertoldsbrunnen – Schwabentorbrücke – Wiehre – **Lorettostrasse**.

(2.8-km, single track with passing loops. A link would be laid between the terminus in Urachstrasse and the route **A** terminus in Günterstalstrasse. An extension beyond Hbf to Lehenerstrasse was included in the plan)

C: Hbf – Bertoldsbrunnen – Schwabentorbrücke – **Bleicheweg**.

(1.1-km, single track branch from route **B** with passing loops). Extensions beyond Bleicheweg to Waldsee and also to Lehenerstrasse were included in the plan)

D: Rennweg – Siegesdenkmal – Bertoldsbrunnen – Lorettostrasse – Wonnhalde – **Günterstal**.

(5.1-km, double track to Lorettostrasse then single track with one passing loop to Günterstal)

Headways would be 5 minutes on routes A, B and C and 15 minutes on route D.

Before work could begin however, there were a few problems which needed resolving. Two elegant 13th century gate towers, the *Schwabentor* in Oberlinden on routes B and C and *Martinstor* to the south of Bertoldsbrunnen on routes A and D, had narrow archways which effectively blocked the paths of the proposed routes. The Council decided to cut a second archway beside *Martinstor*, but the situation at *Schwabentor* required the demolition of a private house and the installation of a single outbound track round the base of the tower. In 1913, the house adjoining the opposite side of the tower was purchased and a second archway cut through the ground floor. Both towers exist in this form today and contribute a great deal to the city's charm.

The rolling stock

Thirteen kilometres of track, 56 sets of points and 3 crossings were installed and power was supplied at 550 volts dc near Hbf and in Günterstalstrasse.

Twenty seven 2-axle motor cars were ordered from Waggonfabrik Hannover (HAWA), with electrical equipment from Siemens & Halske. Numbered 1-27 and powered by 2 x 9-kW motors, they were delivered during the summer of 1901. Accommodation was provided for 16 passengers on two wooden, longitudinal bench-type seats with space for a further 14 standing. Power was collected from the overhead via a *Lyrabügel*, an elongated bow collector of a type that was popular with tramway undertakings across mainland Europe. The Freiburg version however, could not be turned but was

The system had to be thoroughly tested before being opened for public operation. Here, Siemens engineers drive motor car 4 and open-sided trailer 30 towards Günterstal on a test run a few days before the official opening. *(collection Kaufhold/Hettinge*

pulled over while still in contact with the overhead wire. The rocker panels were finished in polished teak, which became a prominent feature of the city's trams built before the second world war. Otherwise, they were typical of many other trams produced at the turn of the century.

To support the heavier loadings expected on the Günterstal route, four 2-axle trailers were purchased from HAWA. The first, numbered 28, was built to the same specification as the motor cars, with an enclosed saloon and open platforms. Cars 29-31 were open-sided and intended for use during the busy summer months, when many citizens made their excursions to the forest.

One works car purchased at the outset was a brine trailer, later numbered 204. Built by J.Hellmers of Hamburg, it was pushed ahead of a motor car to clear the winter snow from the rails.

To house the fleet, a depot was built adjacent to the Urachstrasse terminus. It had space for 35 cars on 5 tracks, and a sixth track was provided for maintenance, overhaul and repainting. Facilities such as toilets and changing rooms, were provided in a three-storey administration building alongside the depot.

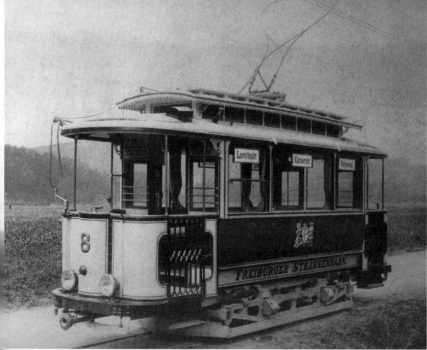

(left) Motor car 8 poses for the camera on the single-track section near Silberbach-strasse, prior to entering service
(collection Kaufhold/Hettinger)

(below) Motor car 21 speeds across Bertoldsbrunnen on a final test run on the morning of the opening day of the system, with the Siemens inspector at the controls. A "tramwagen" on the Hauptbahnhof - Nägeleseestrasse route prepares to cross behind it, 14/10/01. The hand-written inscription on the right of the photgraph was added by the inspector. (collection Kaufhold/Hettinger)

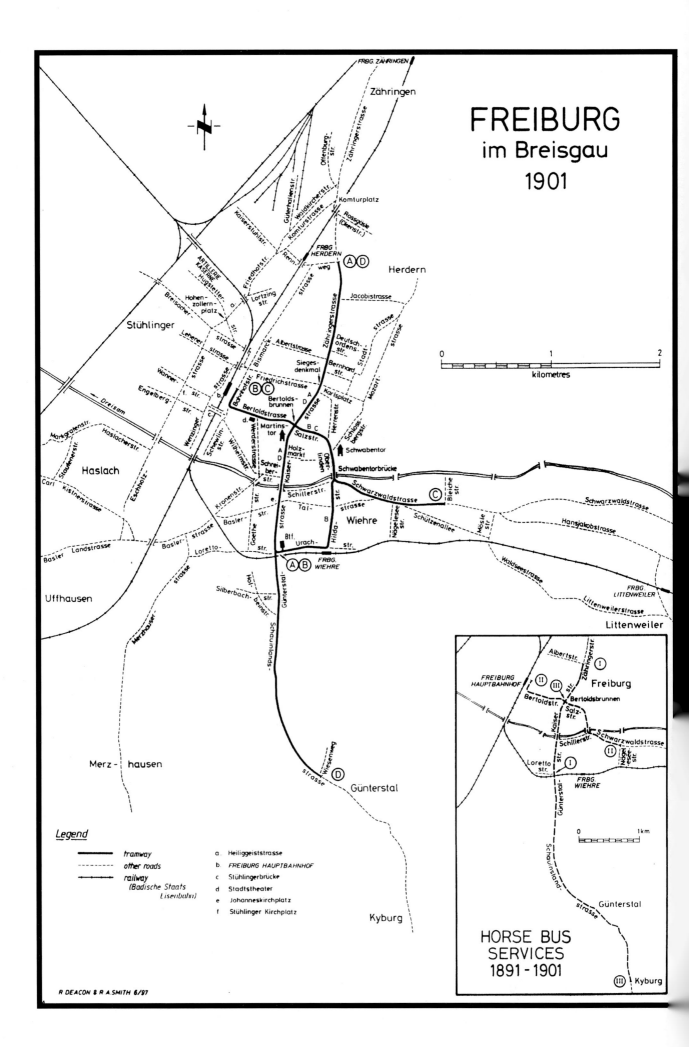

FREIBURG
im Breisgau
1901

FRBG. ZÄHRINGEN

Zähringen

Oftenburg.str.
Zähringerstrasse
Güterhallenstr.
Waldkircherstr.
Komturstrasse
Komturplatz
Rossgässle (Oltenstr.)

Kaiserstuhlstr.
Friedhofstr.

FRBG HERDERN
A D
weg
Herdern

ARTILLERIE KASERNE
Hugsletter
Breisacher
Hohenzollern-platz
Lortzing str.
a.
str.
Jacobistrasse

Stühlinger
Leherer strasse
strasse
Bismarck
Albertstrasse
Zähringerstrasse
Deutsch-ordens.str.
Stadt-
strasse
strasse

Wanner
strasse
Engelberg. str.
Bahnhofstr.
str.
Friedrichstrasse
B C
Siegesdenkmal
Bernhard str.
Mozart.

Oreisam
t. str.
b.
Bertoldsbrunnen
Bertoldstrasse
A D
Karlsplatz
Herrenstr.
Schloss bergstr.

Markgratenstr.
Haslacherstr.
Werzinger
Scheulim str.
Wilhelmstr.
Werderstrasse
d.
c.
Martinstor
Holzmarkt
Salzstr.
B C
Schwabentor

Haslach
Carl Kistnerstrasse
Eschholz-
Kronenstr.
Schreiber-str.
A D
Kaiser-
Ober-
linden
str.
Schillerstr.
Schwabentorbrücke
Schwarzwaldstrasse
C
Bleiche str.
Schwarzwaldstrasse

Staufenstr.
str.
e.
Tal-
strasse
B
Wiehre
Nögelesee str.
Schützenallee
Mösie str.
Hansjakobstrasse

Basler str.
Goethe str.
Btf.
Urach-
Hilda str.
A B
FRBG. WIEHRE

Basler Landstrasse
Basler strasse
Loretto-
Günterstal-
Silberbach-oeinstr.
str.

Uffhausen
Werzhauser
Holz str.
Schaunlands-
Waldseestrasse
Littenweilerstrasse
FRBG. LITTENWEILER

Littenweiler

Merz- hausen
strasse
Wiesenweg
D
Günterstal

Kyburg

Legend

— tramway
-- other roads
+ railway
(Badische Staats Eisenbahn)

a. Heiliggeiststrasse
b. FREIBURG HAUPTBAHNHOF
c. Stühlingerbrücke
d. Stadtstheater
e. Johanneskirchplatz
f. Stühlinger Kirchplatz

Albertstr.
Zähringerstr.
I
FREIBURG HAUPTBAHNHOF
II III
str.
Freiburg
Bertoldstr.
Bertoldsbrunnen
Salz.str.
Kaiser str.
Schillerstr.
Schwarzwaldstrasse
II
Loretto str.
Nögelesee str.
I
FRBG. WIEHRE
Günterstal-
Schaunslard-
strasse
Günterstal
III Kyburg

HORSE BUS
SERVICES
1891-1901

R DEACON & R A.SMITH 6/97

2. Opening and extending the system

Tramway Opening

Thousands of citizens joined in the celebrations that accompanied the opening of the tramway on 14 October 1901. At 11.30 the first decorated tram departed from Bertoldsbrunnen and headed slowly through the crowds towards Günterstal. Brass bands played and people danced and sang in the streets. In the afternoon the line was opened to the public, and every car was filled to capacity.

The opening of the tramway was not the only reason for celebration, however. During the afternoon, the Mayor, Dr Otto Winterer, opened a new *Rathaus* (town hall) and inaugurated the electricity undertaking, by switching on the first electrically-powered street lights.

On the following day routes A and D began operating on 5- and 30-minute headways respectively. As construction around the *Schwabentor* was still in progress, the horse buses operating on this route were given a short reprieve. The last horse bus service departed from Hbf at 21.30 hrs on 27 November 1901 and trams began operating on routes B and C on 2 December. With a 10-minute headway on each route, a 5-minute service was provided on the busy Hbf – Schwabentorbrücke section.

The trams were soon running with full loadings, requiring a 15-minute service to be introduced on route D. By the following summer, demand had reached levels warranting a car every 5 minutes, but the long sections of single track on the Günterstal section prevented further timetable improvements until two further passing loops had been installed.

A flat fare of 10 Pf was charged for single journeys within the city boundary, with a supplement of 5 - 10 Pf for journeys between Lorettostrasse and Günterstal. A multi-ride ticket was available for 1.00 Mark, which entitled the purchaser to 12 single journeys. In 1900, the last full year of horse bus operation, 51 000 passengers were carried, a figure which had risen to 3.25 million in 1902, the first full year of tramway operation.

The Tramway Department was not prepared for the high demand, and cars were often so full it was impossible to board at some places. The purchase of trailers 32-4 from Waggonfabrik Rastatt in 1903 provided some relief. These had enclosed saloon bodies, with open platforms, mounted on 2-axle trucks.

The first extensions

In 1902, the first of the extensions outlined in the original proposal was opened, when routes B and C were extended 200 metres northwards, from Hbf to the junction at Lehenerstrasse. Three years later, route C was extended 800 metres from Bleicheweg to Waldsee, where a turning loop was installed to reduce the damage being caused to the overhead by carelessly-turned bow collectors at the stub termini. Later, in 1905, the single track section from Schwabentorbrücke to Bleicheweg was doubled so that shorter headways could be introduced along this busy corridor.

A short siding was also installed by the Stadttheater for use by special trams carrying late night patrons to their homes in the eastern and southern suburbs. This popular service was extended to northern areas following the installation of a connecting curve at Bertoldsbrunnen.

More trams

To cater for the continual growth in passenger numbers an order was placed with Rastatt for three more trams. Motor cars 28-30 were delivered in 1906, but their bodies were lengthened by 1.4 metres in Urachstrasse depot before entering service, to enable their passenger capacity to be increased to 44. They were mounted on two single-axle, radial-type trucks, a design intended for smooth running on curves, but as they were prone to derailments, were seldom used until modified with conventional 2-axle trucks in 1925.

n early scene depicting three electric cars at the Bertoldsbrunnen crossroads. Car 5 is heading down Kaiserstrasse on route D ,while *e car to the right is preparing to depart on route B or C. The fountain was destroyed in the second world war but the Martinstor gate *wer in the background still survives.

(collection Kaufhold)

Passengers take in the fresh Black Forest air on the open platform of motor car 22 as it passes the Fischerbrunnen and heads alon Kaiser-Joseph-Strasse towards the Siegesdenkmal in the distance, circa 1904. (collection Kaufhol

To avoid duplicating fleet numbers, enclosed 1901 trailer car 28 was renumbered 31" and trailers 29-31 were renumbered 35-7. Three 2-axle trailers delivered by Rastatt in 1907 were numbered 38-40. This rather feeble exercise had to be repeated a few years later, following the delivery of more cars.

More extensions

Following pressure from some of the villages outside the city boundary, the council published proposals for extensions to the tramway in 1906. These included:

Rennweg – Zähringen

(1.7 km, double track extension of routes **A** and **D**.)

Lehernerstrasse – Güterbahnhof

(1.6 km, double track extension of route **C** to the new goods depot.)

Siegesdenkmal – Stühlinger

(A new route to serve this south-west suburb.)

In May 1907, the Council authorised the expenditur of 1.75 million Mark for the construction of the Stühlin ger route and the extensions, the purchase of ten motc + trailer sets to operate the extended services and th erection of a 5-track extension to Urachstrasse depo When this opened in 1908, covered accommodatio was available for 77, 2-axle tramcars.

The *Güterbahnhof* extension was opened before th year was out. The inhabitants of Zähringen on the othe hand, had a much longer wait for the trams to reac them, on account of a low railway bridge north Rossgässle, later renamed Okenstrasse, which neede to be rebuilt before the trams could pass through.

Ten 2-axle motor cars were ordered from MAN of Nürnberg to a similar specification as extended cars 28-30. Numbered 31-40, they arrived in the spring of 1909, and were mounted on two single-axle, radial-type trucks of a new design. MAN also delivered ten 2-axle trailer cars numbered 111-20.

To eliminate the continual renumbering problem every time a new batch of trams arrived, a more logical system was adopted in 1909. Motor cars were numbered in the range 1 to 100, trailers from 101 to 200 and works cars from 201. The trailer cars 31-40 were renumbered 101-10 to conform to the new standard.

Tramway department crews pose proudly in front of motor car 38 at the Waldsee terminus of route 3 in 1910. This car was later preserved at the VKE and DSM museums before returning to Freiburg for restoration by the FFSeV. (collection Kaufhold/Hettinger)

uilt by Rastatt in 1906, motor car 28 was one of three cars to be extensively modified in the tramway's workshops before entering rvice. Their single-axle, radial trucks were replaced by conventional trucks in 1925. The location is Wonnhalde, 1907.
(collection Kaufhold/Hettinger)

Captured outside Urachstrasse depot are water cars (Sprengwagen) 201, mounted on a 2-axle truck, and 202 which, because of size needed two equal-wheel bogies to carry the extra weight. The sprinkler controls are located to the right of the controller.
(collection Kaufhold/Hetting

The first purpose-built, powered works car was also delivered in 1909. Built by Hellmers, number 201 was a 2-axle water sprinkler with a tank capacity of 8 m^2 and was intended for washing the city streets. It was so successful that a second car was purchased three years later. Car 202 was mounted on bogies and had a tank capacity of 12 m^2. The unnumbered brine trailer of 1901 was numbered 204.

Using tramcars to clean the city streets was seen good public relations, so long as care was taken not drench passing pedestrians. Two crewmen we required, one to drive the car and the other to opera the sprinkler controls. They had strict instructions not approach within 50 metres of a car in service when th sprinklers were on, to prevent accidentally sprayir passengers standing on open platforms.

The crew pose in front of motor car 6 at the Herdern terminus of route 6 in 1912. Its newly fitted windscreens required the dash pan to be repositioned at the extreme ends of the underframe.
(collection Kaufhold/Hetting

Change to route numbering

1909 also saw the change from route letters to route numbers and the opening of another route, route 5 from Siegesdenkmal to Stühlinger Kirchplatz, the terminus here being formed by a large loop around the church.

The system now comprised the following routes (former route letters in brackets):

1(A): Komturplatz (Rossgässle) – Bertoldsbrunnen – **Lorettostrasse**

2(D): Komturplatz (Rossgässle) – Bertoldsbrunnen – Lorettostrasse – **Günterstal**

3(C): Güterbahnhof – Hbf – Bertoldsbrunnen – Schwabentorbrücke – **Waldsee**

4(B): Lehenerstrasse – Bertoldsbrunnen – Schwabentorbrücke – **Lorettostrasse**

5: Siegesdenkmal – Hbf – **Stühlinger Kirchplatz**

When the laying of tracks through the reconstructed railway bridge at Rossgässle was completed, the extension to Zähringen was opened on 10 March 1910. The opening ceremony was performed by decorated motor car 34, which was escorted by a large and excited crowd to the new terminus. The headway on route 2 was reduced to 10 minutes and a fare of 15 Pf charged for the journey from Zähringen to Lorettostrasse and 30 Pf for the full journey to Günterstal. A second extension was opened in 1910 when, on 10 December, route 4 was extended across Lorettostrasse to Goethestrasse.

Standing up front on an open platform, exposed to the elements of a bitterly cold Black Forest winter was not the most desirable of occupations. Demands by the drivers for more protection resulted in the fitting of experimental windscreens to motor car 36 in 1910. Work then began on enclosing all of the motor cars, a task that took eight years to complete.

At some time during this period, trailer cars 101, 105-10, were fitted with bow-type current collectors. These were raised to the overhead at stub-end termini, to provide heat and light while the motor car was being shunted from one end of the trailer to the other. The practice continued until 1949, when the collectors were removed.

More extensions proposed

This was a busy period for the tramway, the highlight of which was the publishing of proposals for the following extensions, totalling 8.5 km of route:

Siegesdenkmal – Herdern

1.5 km extension to the village of Herdern.

Schreiberstrasse – Kronenstrasse

First phase for two planned new routes; St Georgen and Merzhausen.

Stühlinger Kirchplatz – Haslach

1.8 km extension to the village of Haslach.

Stühlinger Kirchplatz – Hohenzollernplatz

1 km single track line connecting routes 3 and 5, the initial part of a long-term objective for a new route from Haslach to Güterbahnhof.

Hohenzollernplatz – Artilleriekaserne

0.9 km extension of route 4, included at the request of the army.

Hohenzollernplatz – Betzenhausen

At 2.8 km, the longest of the proposed extensions, running single track to the outlying farming community. It was later removed from the list because of its high construction costs and anticipated low return.

Although the system was heavily used, it continued to lose money. Such was the concern over the tramway's finances that the number of new extensions was reduced to two; to Herdern and Haslach, a total of 3.3 km. When the line to Haslach opened on 1 October 1913, route 5 was extended from Stühlinger Kirchplatz. On 1 July 1914, the extension from Siegesdenkmal to Herdern began operating as new route 6.

Additional rolling stock began arriving in the spring of 1914 and comprised seven motor cars numbered 41-47. Built by MAN, they were similar to the 1909 batch except for the fitting of conventional 2-axle trucks and were put to work on route 2 (Zähringen – Günterstal).

Schauinsland Eisenbahn - the first proposals

Construction of a new double-track section of tramway on route 2 between Silberbachstrasse and Wiesenweg began in 1913. Built over open country on private-right-of-way, it was planned as the first section of a high speed tramway to the terminus of a proposed mountain railway at Friedrichshof, 4 km south east of Günterstal. A study by a consultant from Zürich had confirmed the feasibility of building a rack railway, over the *Heibrainkopf* and *Holzschlägermatte* ridges, to the summit at Schauinsland. Rolling stock would comprise trains of motor and trailers, the trailers being detached at Friedrichshof and coupled to route 2 motor cars for the final part of the journey to the city. The procedure would be reversed when travelling in the opposite direction.

The City Council, meanwhile, was busy studying proposals from companies offering a variety of solutions for transporting large numbers of people to the mountains. Three were based on rack railways and four on suspended cable cars. One of the latter, submitted by Professor Benoit of Karlsruhe Technical University, described a 2.7-km aerial cableway, operated with suspended cabins, offering a capacity of 250-300 passengers per hour. An eighth proposal, promoted by *Daimler Motoren Gesellschaft*, was for a trolleybus route. No further trolleybus proposal was seen in Freiburg until just before world war 2.

The most promising proposal however, submitted by the Darmstadt-based *Süddeutsche Eisenbahn-Gesellschaft* (SEG), was for a 35-km adhesion railway, to be built in three phases:

Phase 1: From Freiburg Hbf, running via Merzhausen and Au, through the Hexental valley to Horben.

Phase 2: From Horben, up and over Schauinsland and Notschrei to Todtnau where connection would be made to the *Zell – Todtnauer Bahn* (ZTB). This would be purchased by the SEG and electrified.

Phase 3: A branch from Notschrei via Feldberg to Sankt Blasien.

Freiburg Council proposed the formation of an independent *Freiburger Eisenbahn Gesellschaft AG* and agreement was reached on 20 July 1914 for construction of the first phase of the *Schauinsland Eisenbahn*. The outbreak of war however, prevented a start on its construction.

When hostilities ceased, valiant attempts were made to reactivate the project, but to no avail. Had it materialised, the region might now be reaping the benefit of its own "little Switzerland", with trains climbing through colourful plateaus and beautiful scenery. Chapter 4 describes how a "Benoit" type cable car line was eventually built in its place.

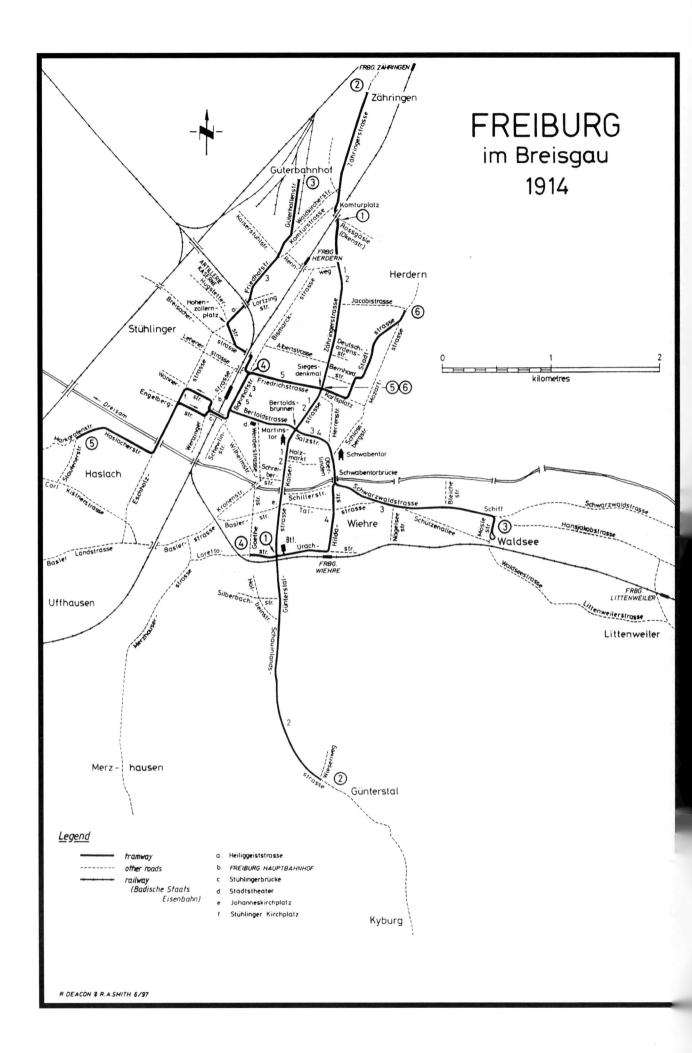

FREIBURG
im Breisgau
1914

Zähringen

Güterbahnhof

Herdern

Stühlinger

Haslach

Wiehre

Waldsee

Uffhausen

Littenweiler

Merz – hausen

Günterstal

Kyburg

FRBG. ZÄHRINGEN

Komturplatz
Rossgässle (Okenstr.)

FRBG HERDERN

Jacobistrasse

Siegesdenkmal

Friedrichstrasse

Bertoldsbrunnen

Bertoldstrasse

Martinstor

Schwabentor

Schwabentorbrücke

Schiff

FRBG. WIEHRE

FRBG. LITTENWEILER

0   1   2
kilometres

Legend

	tramway	a.	Heiliggeiststrasse
	other roads	b.	FREIBURG HAUPTBAHNHOF
	railway	c.	Stühlingerbrücke
	(Badische Staats	d.	Stadtstheater
	Eisenbahn)	e.	Johanneskirchplatz
		f.	Stühlinger Kirchplatz

R. DEACON & R.A.SMITH 6/97

3. World War 1 and the early-'twenties

War breaks out

When war broke out on 1 August 1914, the tram fleet stood at 47 motor cars, 20 trailers and 4 works cars, operating on 6 routes over 17.8 km of track. Work on expanding the tramway was stopped, including the laying of new tracks on the Günterstal line. By 1915, all but 9 of the 133 male drivers and conductors had departed for military duties, causing a severe shortage of staff. Women were employed for the first time and by 1917 there were 70 female drivers and 30 conductresses.

Routes 4 and 5 were withdrawn during the early months of the conflict, but redundant trams were not kept idle. Trailer cars 113-16 were converted for use as ambulances by the Red Cross, transporting wounded soldiers from *Güterbahnhof* to military hospitals around the city. A section of track was laid from Kaiserstuhlstrasse to provide direct access to the railway loading ramp. As the flow of casualties increased, up to twelve ambulance trams could be seen waiting for the hospital trains. Over 77 000 wounded soldiers were transported from *Güterbahnhof* by this means.

The first serious accident involving a tram occurred on 12 October 1916, when motor car 32 was hit by a train on the *Höllentalbahn* railway crossing in Günterstalstrasse. It was returning from Günterstal at 21.30, in complete darkness on a rainy evening, when it crashed through the barrier as the train approached. Fortunately, there were only three people on the tram, one passenger who, together with the conductor, was slightly injured, and the driver who was more seriously hurt. Car 32 was badly damaged and was scrapped soon after.

Shortages of manpower and materials began to have a serious impact on the running of the tramway. As spares became depleted, defective cars were stripped to keep others in serviceable condition, and trams were often pressed into passenger service with major defects, such as running on one motor. Work on the permanent way was limited to emergency repairs only.

To make matters worse, the army commandeered some of the trams to move its personnel and equipment around the city. Open-sided trailers 102-4 were adapted to carry goods, and a second spur was installed into *Güterbahnhof* to speed up the transfer of equipment. The requisitioned trams continued their military role until the end of hostilities.

After the war

At the end of the war the tramway was in a perilous state. A shortage of coal had reduced the production of electricity, causing a restriction in the number of trams in service. By November 1918, a 20-minute headway was all that could be operated and some journeys terminated short to conserve electricity supplies.

Over the next few years the city slowly returned to a peacetime lifestyle akin to prewar standards. In the summer of 1921, a revised route network saw routes 3 and 4 exchanging termini, and route 5 operating a through service between Herdern and Haslach. Route 6 became a short feeder service operating between Schwabentorbrücke and Goethestrasse.

In 1922, rising inflation began to take its toll. Public spending was cut and prices rose sharply. Route 6 was an early casualty when it was 'temporarily' closed in October – it did not reopen until December 1924.

To keep pace with rising inflation, which gradually assumed monstrous proportions throughout Germany, new fare tariffs were introduced with monotonous regularity. In 1919, the cost of a tram ticket varied between 15 and 25 Pf depending on the length of the journey. By the following year, this had more than doubled to a flat

This 1916 photograph shows motor car 45 at the Rössgassle terminus of route 1, with a female crew. On withdrawal from works duties 1972, car 45 was preserved at the VKE and DSM museums, before returning to Freiburg where it is currently undergoing restoration the FFSeV.
(collection Kaufhold/Hettinger)

rate of 60 Pf for all journeys. At the end of 1921 it had reached 1.50 Mark, and in 1922 fares were raised no less than 15 times, to 300 Mark per journey. The highest tariff was charged in November 1923, when passengers travelling between Hbf and Bertoldsbrunnen paid a staggering 100 milliard (1 milliard=1000 000 000) Mark. It was no surprise therefore, that this period recorded the lowest number of daily passenger journeys: 2203 on the last day of November.

Emil Eitner, who in 1926 was still the Director of the tramway, wrote in an account celebrating its 25th anniversary, that it had come perilously close to being abandoned in 1923, and was saved only by the revaluation of the Mark. A new fare tariff was introduced with a single ticket costing 20 *Neue Pfennige* and a booklet of 10 single tickets was available for 1.30 Mark.

Motor car 31 on the route 4 extension at the Littenweiler terminus. The single-axle radial trucks on this batch of cars were replaced by conventional 2-axle trucks in the late 'thirties.   (collection Kaufhold/Hettinger)

Maximum-traction car 61 poses at Wonnhalde in 1929, soon after delivery from Rastatt.   (collection Kaufhold/Hetting)

4. Expanding the system

New trams, but also new bus routes

With the crisis years of war and inflation behind it, construction began in 1924 of a 1.85 km extension of route 4 from Schiff via Hansjakobstrasse and Lindenmattenstrasse to the village of Littenweiler. The first section was opened as far as Hammerschmiedstrasse in December, with the final section to Littenweiler Bahnhof opening on 7 March 1925. From the same day, route 3 was extended from Bleichestrasse to Waldsee.

In Haslach, on the other side of the city, a 250-metre extension of route 5, was opened between Markgrafenstrasse and Schulhaus on 10 April 1925.

Sensing that the time was right, the councils of St Georgen, Merzhausen and Betzenhausen resubmitted requests for tramway extensions to their villages, and their pleas were not entirely unheeded. As the motorbus was being promoted as a more cost-effective solution for rural routes and was appearing in increasing numbers across the country, it was no surprise that the bus was selected to connect these and some of the other outlying villages to the city's growing transport network.

A fierce anti-tram campaign, led by the *Freiburger Zeitung*, persuaded Herr Eitner to modernise the fleet. An order was placed for ten bogie motor cars, which for political reasons, was divided between two manufacturers: 47-52 from Fuchs of Heidelberg, and 53-6 from Rastatt. They arrived in 1927 and were identical except for the type of current collectors fitted. The Fuchs cars had *Scheren* type pantographs, built of rectangular rod frames and looking rather dated, while the Rastatt cars were fitted with the standard *Lyrabügel*. These were replaced by *Scheren* collectors in the following year.

At 11.10 metres, these handsome cars were the longest in the fleet. Their rocker panels were finished in traditional varnished teak, and the interiors tastefully furnished in mahogany and teak. Mounted on maximum-traction trucks, they were powered by 2 x 37-kW motors and had capacity for 26 seated and 24 standing passengers.

Even before they arrived, Urachstrasse depot was suffering an acute shortage of space, with up to 18 trams being stabled overnight in the forecourt. Eitner purchased a piece of land in Komturstrasse in the north of the city, and built a five-track depot, big enough to accommodate 30 trams. It was connected to the system via a new double track tramway, which was laid between Kaiserstuhlstrasse and the Zähringen route at Komturplatz. When the depot opened on 8 May 1928, route 4 was extended along Komturstrasse to Komturplatz. On the same day, route 1 was extended from Rossgässle to Komturplatz. The system now comprised the following routes:-

1: **Komturplatz – Lorettostrasse**
2: **Zähringen – Günterstal**
3: **Hohenzollernplatz – Schiff**
4: **Komturplatz – Littenweiler**
5: **Herdern – Haslach**
6: **Schwabentorbrücke – Goethestrasse**

elivered by Rastatt as number 39 in 1907, trailer car 109 attracts the attention of a passing cyclist as it crosses the Kaiserbrücke in 930. The bow collector fitted to the trailer was raised at termini to maintain lighting and heating while the motor car shunted from one nd to the other.

(Gebr. Metz)

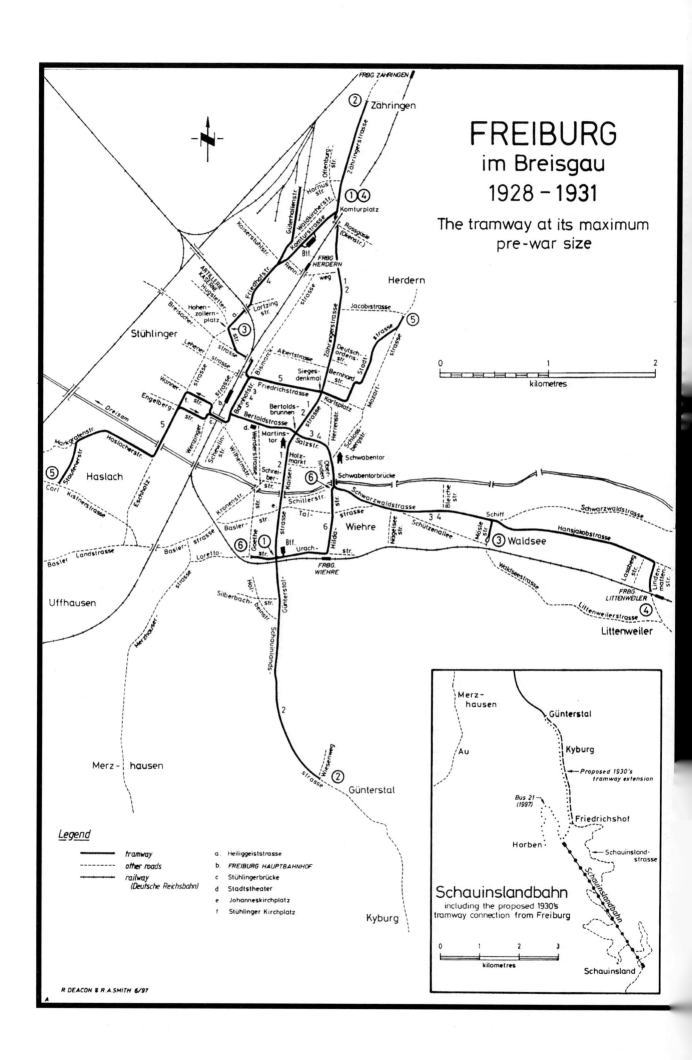

FREIBURG
im Breisgau
1928 – 1931

The tramway at its maximum
pre-war size

FRBG ZÄHRINGEN

② Zähringen

① ④ Komturplatz

Rossgässle
(Okenstr.)

FRBG
HERDERN

Herdern

Jacobistrasse

⑤

Bf.

ARTILLERIE
KASERNE

Stühlinger

③

Siegesdenkmal

Deutschordensstr.

Bernhardstr.

5

Friedrichstrasse

Bertoldsbrunnen

Martinstor

Karlsplatz

Schwabentor

3 4

⑥ Schwabentorbrücke

Schwarzwaldstrasse

Schiff

Schwarzwaldstrasse

Hansjakobstrasse

⑤ Haslach

Schillerstr.

6 Wiehre

3 4

③ Waldsee

Dreisam

⑥ ①

Bf.

FRBG
WIEHRE

FRBG
LITTENWEILER

④

Uffhausen

Littenweiler

Merz- hausen

② Günterstal

Kyburg

Legend

————— tramway
- - - - - other roads
┼┼┼┼┼┼ railway
          (Deutsche Reichsbahn)

a. Heiliggeiststrasse
b. FREIBURG HAUPTBAHNHOF
c. Stühlingerbrücke
d. Stadtstheater
e. Johanneskirchplatz
f. Stühlinger Kirchplatz

0   1   2
kilometres

Merz-
hausen

Au

Günterstal

Kyburg

← Proposed 1930's
   tramway extension

Bus 21
(1997)

Horben

Friedrichshof

Schauinslandstrasse

Schauinslandbahn
including the proposed 1930's
tramway connection from Freiburg

0   1   2   3
kilometres

Schauinsland

R.DEACON & R.A.SMITH 6/97

Looking south towards the forested hills. The twin spires of the Johanneskirche look down on this tranquil scene at the Kaiserbrücke in 1926. The two trams have the monopoly of the roadway. (collection Kaufhold/Hettinger)

In 1929, a third and final batch of maximum-traction motor cars was purchased from Rastatt. Numbered 57-61, they were also the last cars to be built to Freiburg's own specifications and differed from the previous batches by having a five-bay instead of six-bay saloon.

The *Schauinslandbahn* as a *Seilschwebebahn*

By now, work was well advanced on construction of the world's pioneering passenger-carrying, suspension cable car line, climbing from Friedrichshof (468 metres) to Gipfels (1214 metres). An intermediate station was built for the convenience of people wishing to walk in the forest. Using one carrying cable and two traction cables on the Benoit principle, the 3.6-km, privately-operated line, was opened on 17 July 1930.

Ten cars were purchased, each with a capacity of 22 passengers and a conductor. Travelling at 5 m/sec on a 5-minute headway, operating with two cars, 88 passengers per hour could be carried in each direction. During busy periods, up to eight cars could be operated at any one time, raising the line's capacity to 330 passengers per hour, per direction.

Apart from one fatal accident in 1932, the system worked smoothly through the war and up until 1964/5, when the electrical equipment was replaced and new driving control gear installed at the top station. Freiburg became the owner in 1968 and it was absorbed into the *Freiburger Verkehrs AG* in 1982, but retained its own fare system.

In 1986, by which time the line was losing DEM 1 million a year, it was decided to reduce the total staff from 16 to 8, by installing ticket machines, and rebuilding the line for operation with 37 Swiss-built, 7-passenger cabins. 40 percent of the modernisation cost was borne by the *Land*. In October 1987, the line closed to allow work to commence on the complete renewal of the infrastructure. It reopened on 6 December 1988.

During periods of high demand, up to 30 cabins can be run on the cable, giving a maximum capacity of 680 passengers. "Clusters" of three or four cabins on a short span of cable, are a common sight.

The line is one of the longest cable car lines in Europe and climbs through 746 metres of wooded mountainside, affording stunning views of the surrounding forests, the city of Freiburg, the Rhine basin and the Vosges mountains of the Alsace region of France beyond.

A new proposal for trams to Friedrichshof

Buoyed by the success of the cable car, the tramway department published a proposal for an extension of route 2 to Friedrichshof. The service would be operated by motor and trailer sets from the city as far as Günterstal, where the trailers would be uncoupled, leaving the motor cars to run solo to Friedrichshof. Returning motor cars would attach a trailer at Günterstal before completing the journey back to the city. A small depot would be built in Günterstal to house five cars. Although well supported, the cost could not be justified, and a feeder bus service was introduced instead.

In 1931, the *Reichsbahn* (state railway) began construction of a new section of line, partly in tunnel, to reroute the *Höllentalbahn* away from the busy level crossing in Günterstalstrasse. This led to the closure of the section of tram route 6 between Goethestrasse and Lorettostrasse from 15 October. A new station to serve the Wiehre area was opened on 8 November 1934, some distance from the tramway, but with no money to reroute the line, route 6 was replaced by buses from the same date. The tracks between Urachstrasse and Schwabentorbrücke remained in use for depot workings, on which passengers could be carried.

The single-axle radial trucks on motor cars 31-9 were never successful and, following a serious accident involving car 38, the complete batch was re-fitted with conventional Rastatt 2-axle trucks between 1936 and 1940. Also during this period, trailer cars 114/5 received fully-enclosed platforms and the complete batch (cars 111-20) were equipped with bow-type current collectors to provide lighting and heating at the termini.

Preparing for World War 2

With the rapidly changing political scene in Germany during this period, and the rise of the National Socialist party, advertisements and slogans began to appear at every vantage point. In Freiburg, Johannes-Kirchplatz was renamed "Danziger Freiheit" and Kaiserstrasse became "Adolf Hitler Strasse" (both reverting to their original names after World War 2). Motor car 13 was adorned with slogans and driven round the city to promote the cause. Across the nation, public transport received much acclaim for moving millions of supporters to the numerous rallies across the country. In 1935, newspaper headlines proclaimed that 400 million people travelled by bus, 1000 million by train and 2600 million by tram to the various political events.

Freiburg contributed 9.4 million tram passengers, a figure that had grown to 9.8 million by 1938. A local newspaper stated that *Freiburgers* preferred to travel by tram and that Freiburg's trams travelled a distance equivalent to that from Freiburg to Berlin every day. It concluded, "*that on average, seventy percent of the city's 103 200 inhabitants make at least one tram journey per day*". The rallies and celebrations continued until the outbreak of World War 2 in 1939.

What better way to promote your cause than on a roving public transport vehicle. Here, motor car 13 is seen in the late 'thirties outside Urachstrasse depot bearing slogans for the National Socialist party and a map depicting a future "Gross Deutschland".
(collection Kaufhold/Hettinger)

5. World War 2 and devastation

Wartime restrictions

Following the outbreak of war in September 1939, restrictions similar to those imposed during the first world war, were brought back into force. This included the introduction of fuel rationing which brought about the withdrawal of most of the city's bus services. The cuts in the tram services involved combining routes 1 with 2 and 3 with 4, operated with solo motor cars only.

Although fewer trams were running, they were expected to carry increasing numbers of passengers. A few extra trams were run during busy periods and trailers appeared on route 3/4, but demand continually outstripped supply. A press campaign for the restoration of services to prewar levels met with limited success when route 6 was reintroduced between Schwabentorbrücke and Lorettostrasse on 12 February 1940. The tracks here had been kept for depot workings.

The motor cars in the series 1-27 were slow in traffic and tended to delay the faster cars. To improve running times, 43 of the 101 tram stops were removed to enable the slower cars to maintain their maximum speeds for longer periods.

Trolleybuses (almost)

Shortly before the war, Siemens-Schuckert of Berlin had prepared a proposal for a trolleybus route running from Zähringen, northwards through open country to the villages of Emmendingen and Waldkirch, but the City Council rejected it. As the war progressed however, and fuel became impossible to obtain, the transport department decided to install two trolleybus routes, from the city centre to Haslach and St Georgen. As the exact routes are unknown they are not shown on any map. Work began in August 1944 on the erection of overhead standards, and six trolleybuses were ordered from *Omnibus Bedarfs GmbH*, but they were never delivered, as an allied air raid destroyed much of the city, and with it the prospect of introducing trolleybuses.

Freiburg bombed

At 20.00 on the evening of 27 November 1944, heavy bombers devastated the central area of the city, and 2700 people lost their lives. Several trams operating on route 3/4 were destroyed or damaged beyond repair. Motor car 53 and trailer 110 were gutted by fire near Stadttheater; motor car 44 and trailer 107 were badly damaged outside Hbf and later scrapped; motor car 1 was destroyed in Kaiserstuhlstrasse; motor cars 9 and 22 were destroyed in other parts of the city and sister car 7 was found to be beyond repair and scrapped. Twenty-six other cars received minor damage and were repaired or rebuilt.

Approximately 900 metres of track was destroyed and fifty percent of overhead brought down, mostly in the centre, and to the north and west. The only sections to remain intact were those between Holzmarkt and Günterstal on route 2 and Oberlinden and Littenweiler on route 4. As both sections were accessible from Urachstrasse depot, skeleton services were soon running on these two routes. Permanent way gangs were meanwhile salvaging equipment from the outer ends of route 5 to repair the damaged sections of routes 2 and 4.

On 15 April 1945, French troops occupied the Freiburg area and closed the tramway system down.

Most of the waiting passengers have managed to cram on board open-balconied trailer 120 and maximum-traction motor car 47, prior to their departure from Bertoldsbrunnen for Zähringen on route 2 in 1947. Note the bow collector fitted to the trailer. (K.Müller)

(left) This view, looking east from Bertoldsbrunnen, captures motor car 38 passing the devasted buildings in Salzstrasse while operating a route 3 service to Hauptbahnhof during the summer of 1946
                                                (K.Müller)

The Hauptbahnhof lies in ruins and passengers board trams on routes 3 and 4 in the summer of 1946. Maximum-traction motor car looks in remarkably good condition, but trailer 108 bears all the hallmarks of wartime neglect.
                                                (K.Mülle

6. Rebuilding and modernisation

Restoration of services

As soon as peace was established, the citizens of Freiburg began the long and arduous task of clearing the rubble away, restoring public services and rebuilding their shattered city. The two shuttle tram services were able to start running again on routes 2 and 4 on 10-minute headways on 26 May 1945, between 07.00 and 20.00.

Within a month, repairs were completed on the 800 metres of overhead between Rennweg and Friedrich-Ebert-Platz (formerly Hohenzollernplatz), and on the tracks and overhead in Lortzingstrasse and Friedrich-Ebert-Platz. This enabled a third shuttle service to start operating on the section between Zähringen and Friedrich-Ebert-Platz from 25 June. Rolling stock was provided from Komturstrasse depot, running on a 12-minute headway.

In August, permanent way gangs moved into the area bounded by Deutschordenstrasse, Bernhardstrasse and Siegesdenkmal, to enable through-running to resume on route 2. This occurred on 4 October.

The restoration of the tramway could not commence on the western side of the city because of demolition and clearance work. This demoralising task continued throughout the winter until February 1946, when trams were able to start running between Littenweiler and Komturplatz, via Hbf.

On route 5, the Stühlingerbrücke, which carried the tram tracks over the main railway line near Hbf, was badly damaged, and most of the usable overhead equipment had been removed from this route to carry out repairs on the trunk routes. As more trams became available, the route 6 shuttle was reopened between Lorettostrasse and Schwabentorbrücke.

Returning evacuees placed a heavy burden on the depleted transport system. The trams were so overcrowded during rush-hours that passengers clung on to anything they could grab hold of. As conductors were unable to pass through the overcrowded cars, fare evasion (Schwarzfahren) became something of a sport.

Although finance was scarce, the Strassenbahn Direktor, now Herr Bachert, obtained funding for limited modernisation of the tram fleet. Work began in 1949 to fit 60-kW motors and railbrakes to some of the maximum-traction cars, car 60 being the first to receive the new equipment. As a demonstration of the increase in performance, a "tram race" was held with sister car 61 on the double-track section of route 2 between Wonnhalde and Wiesenweg. With the Mayor and members of the Council on board, car 60 left 61 trailing in its wake. The displaced motors from the modified cars were subsequently fitted to motor cars 34/6/8/41/3.

The Scheren current collectors on the maximum-traction cars were replaced with more modern pantographs and the displaced collectors fitted to some of the surviving motor cars in the batch 2-27.

In 1949-50, trailer cars 108/9/11/4-20 were rebodied by Waggonfabrik Rathgeber of München, and renumbered 116-25. Their return to service heralded a desperately needed improvement in comfort, and passenger capacity was increased to 70. The permanent way received further attention and, after the last section of bomb-damaged track was repaired, route 5 began operating between Herdern and Haslach on 15 April 1949.

New standard cars

With the gradual relaxation of restrictions on the supply of raw materials, eleven 2-axle motor cars and nine

ʌx of the 1949/50 rebodied trailers, headed by 122, are seen lined-up outside Komturstrasse Btf, while a works car goes about its ʌeryday business in the background.
(collection Kaufhold/Hettinger)

By 1949, many of the city's prewar social and sporting activities had been reinstated. Here in Kaiser-Joseph-Strasse, the flags are flying to mark the running of the Schauinsland hill climb, and motor car 46 and trailer are carrying spectators to the connecting bus service at Günterstal.
(K.Müller)

With curtains half drawn to protect its passengers from the heat of the sun, motor car 39 is caught on camera on route 5, 8/51.
(J.G.Gilham)

trailers were ordered from Rastatt and Rathgeber respectively, to the new national standard *Verbandstyp* specification. Many such cars were produced by various manufacturers and they were undoubtedly responsible for the survival of many systems to the present day.

Construction of an extension to Komturstrasse depot for the new trams began late in 1948. *Halle III* as it was called, opened on 15 April 1950, and contained six storage tracks, enough to house 48 *Verbandstyp* tramcars. Built adjacent to Komturstrasse, it had access from both ends. From the same day, the operation of routes based at Urachstrasse depot, along with its passenger cars, drivers and conductors, were transferred to Komturstrasse. Thereafter, Urachstrasse's role became that of a central works, with five works cars and 36 staff.

To cater for the increasing number of people using Wiehre Bahnhof, route 6 was replaced by buses on 19 November 1950. The tracks between Urachstrasse depot and Schwabentorbrücke remained in use for the theatre *specials* and depot workings until 27 November 1959.

The nine *Verbandstyp* trailers were allocated fleet numbers 126-34 and began arriving in the summer of 1950. Delivery of the motor cars 61-71 commenced early in 1951. They were painted cream with a green waist line, the most common postwar tramcar livery in Germany. Maximum-traction car 61 of 1929 was renumbered 53", the original car bearing this number having been destroyed in the war, and the remaining 1901-built 2-axle cars were withdrawn from passenger service.

Maximum-traction motor car 54 heads along Konstanz Road on route 3 in August 1951. It would appear that passengers were allowed to ride alongside the driver in those days.
(J.G.Gilham)

The track layout at Komturplatz has changed several times over the years to accommodate increasing traffic demands. This circa 1950 view captures maximum-traction motor car 49 with trailers 113" (with open platforms) and 115", preparing to depart for Lorettostrasse on route 1.
(Collection Kaufhold/Hettinger)

A brand new three-car Verbandstyp set, comprising motor car 73 and trailers 142 and 141, poses for the camera near Wonnhalde soon after being delivered from Rastatt in 1953. *(collection VAG)*

On 1 July 1951, route 5 was extended 200 metres at Herdern and the track in Eschholzstrasse doubled in the following year. Plans to double the track on the southern section to Haslach were cancelled through lack of money.

Finance was provided however, for three more *Verbandstyp* motor cars and nine trailers, and these were delivered by Rastatt in 1953. The motor cars were numbered 72-4 and the trailers 135-43.

A further increase in passenger capacity was provided by converting 1901-built motor cars, 3/4/6/10/8/25/6, to trailers and renumbering them 105"-11". Cars 12/4/5/7/20/1/5/7, were adapted for works duties and 2/6/11/3 were designated advertising cars. Car 2 was subsequently retained by the VAG as a museum car.

A major upgrading of route 2 between Holbeinstrasse and Wiesenweg began in 1954, with barrier protection, paved waiting islands and passenger shelters at each

"Sputnik" 100 during a break at Komturstrasse Btf while undergoing acceptance testing in October 1959. Withdrawn from passenger service in 1994, it became an advertising car and is the only surviving example of these first generation articulated cars.

(collection Kaufhold)

The last year of operation on route 5 is depicted in this view of maximum-traction motor cars 49 and 51 at the Haslach terminus in the summer of 1961.   *(collection Kaufhold/Hettinger)*

tram stop. The work was spread over several years and resulted in a smooth, fast, suburban light rail line. At the other end of the system, a turning circle was installed at Komturplatz in 1956, for use by routes 1 and 4.

To ease the continual overcrowding, three *Verbandstyp*-styled, single-ended, 4-axle articulated trams were ordered from Rastatt. Designed for passenger flow, with a conductor's desk, ticket and cash dispenser inside the rear entrance, these were Freiburg's first articulated cars. The front body section was mounted on a 2-axle rigid truck, which housed the 2 x 60-kW motors, and the rear section on an unpowered bogie, a configuration commonly known as *Sattelschlepper* in Germany (which loosely translates to tractor and trailer – as in an articulated lorry).

Numbered 100-2, they began to arrive in October 1959 and entered service on route 4. The *"Sputniks"* as they affectionately became known (1959 was the year of the first manned space flight), were 17.43 metres long and could carry 42 seated and 100 standing passengers. Capacity was increased to 212 when a *Verbandstyp* trailer was attached. During their subsequent conversion for one-man operation, the conductor's desk was removed, allowing an extra 18 passengers (39 seated and 121 standing in all) to be carried in a single car.

A reversing triangle was installed at Littenweiler Bahnhof to enable the *"Sputniks"* to turn, but the line was cut back a short distance to a newly-installed turning circle at Lassbergstrasse on 21 December 1964. Route 3 was extended to Littenweiler from the same date to provide extra capacity on this busy route.

Several older cars were now surplus to requirements and withdrawn for scrap. These included the last two 1907-built motor cars, 28/9, 1909-built motor cars 33/5/7/9, 1903-built trailers 112/3, and the seven trailers, 105-11, converted from motor cars in 1954.

More closures and more modern cars

Despite the recent modernisation, the decision was taken to close route 5, which ran between Haslach and Herdern. The reasons given were that the cost of doubling the single track sections and replacing the old rolling stock could not be justified. A critical factor however, was the impending construction of *Bundesstrasse 31*, which would sever the route north of Haslach and require extensive diversions to keep it running. Tram route 5 ran for the last time on 31 December 1961.

In an attempt to appease public hostility to the closure, the transport department published proposals for an extension northwards to a convenient point for a turning circle in Zähringen, and a southerly extension through Günterstal to connect with the Schauinsland cable-car feeder bus service. It is interesting to note that twenty years were to pass before the extension through Günterstal materialised. The Zähringen extension is still awaited.

The growing affluence in postwar Germany saw more cars on the roads and notable increases in congestion, particularly in the cities. Peak-hour surveys at Bertoldsbrunnen found that an average of 9000 passengers per hour were using the four tram routes, and concluded that road space for an additional 3600 vehicles would be required if they decided to travel by car instead. It concluded that if current ridership levels were to be maintained and more people tempted out of their cars on to public transport, drastic measures would need to be taken.

Replacement of the trams by buses was the solution promoted by an anti-tram group, which took every opportunity to blame the trams for the congestion. Experience elsewhere in Germany however, had demonstrated that intelligent traffic management, based on a segregated tramway, actually eased congestion. This had a profound effect on the thinking in Freiburg, where the decision was taken to extend and modernise the system, with high capacity tramcars running on private rights-of-way, with priority at major road intersections.

Around this time, the *Stuttgarter Strassenbahn AG*, in collaboration with *Maschinenfabrik Esslingen*, was busy developing a 4-axle, two section, single-ended articulated tramcar for the city's metre-gauge tramway. A conventional type articulation unit was ruled out because of the steep winding roads that predominate. The specification defined a vehicle 2.20 metres wide, 18 metres long, and able to carry 160 passengers with a ratio of three standing to one seated. The result was a handsome and rugged vehicle ideally suited for the Stuttgart terrain.

Despite the unorthodox design, no prototype was built, probably because of Esslingen's excellent reputation in the tramcar construction industry. Stuttgart 501, the first production car, was unveiled to the press in 1959. Mounted on two 2-axle trucks located towards the outer ends of the body sections, it was powered by 2 x 100-kW Garbe Lahmeyer motors, and carried on a subframe which supported both the body sections and articulation unit. The two inner axles were driven via cardan shafts. AEG and Kiepe supplied the electrical equipment which was fitted to the underside of the body sections and the subframe.

Rheostatic braking was used to bring the car to a virtual stop, and four electromagnetic rail brakes, two per bogie, provided emergency braking. Once stopped, the car was prevented from moving by drum brakes fitted to each axle.

Stuttgart took delivery of 350 of these splendid cars between 1959 and 1965 and many were subsequently modified for operation in "double traction". Reutlingen bought 3 double-ended examples in 1963, and Neunkirchen 8 double-ended, standard-gauge variants in 1961. It is appropriate to note that in later years, as the Stuttgart system converted to standard gauge, many of its GT4 cars were sold on to the systems operating in Augsburg, Halberstadt, Halle, Nordhausen, Ulm, and Arad in Romania.

Freiburg sent a delegation to Stuttgart to inspect them and, having been suitably impressed, an order was placed for six double-ended versions. They were allocated fleet numbers 103-8 and their delivery spread over six months, so that the Freiburg cars could be slipped into the Stuttgart production schedule. Siemens supplied the electrical equipment and motors, which were noticeably quieter than the Stuttgart variant. They were painted in a cream livery with an olive green waist band.

The first Esslingen built GT4 for Freiburg, car 103", at Komturstrasse depot during acceptance testing in July 1962. Withdrawn in 1997 and currently numbered 109, it forms part of the growing collection of preserved cars in the city. (W.Pragher)

With the arrival of the first GT4 cars the remaining 2-axle cars were withdrawn. Car 36 passes through Obe linden, one of the most pleasant areas of the inner city, while on its way to Emil-Gött-Strasse in 1960. Th fountain, Bächle and Münster are clearly visible as is the famous "Roten Bären" inn on the left. (K.Mülle

The Verbandstyp cars were a common sight in the city for three decades. Here we see(top) motor car 74 and trailer 142 on route 4 alongside sister car 65 operating the 1966 VDVA tour of the system, at the Littenweiler terminus. The lower photograph, taken at the same location, depicts one of the attractive little Rathgeber trailers, number 127 behind motor car 70, 4/8/66.

(collection Kaufhold/Hettinger)

The entry into service of the Rastatt-built GT4 cars saw the demise of the maximum-traction cars. Here we see cars 50 and 51 on the Möslestrasse (Stadthalle) turning loop while operating as extras, 5/3/67. *(collection Kaufhold)*

Capacity was provided for 37 seated passengers and 118 standing. The first three arrived in July 1962 and were assigned to the Zähringen – Günterstal route, where they could demonstrate their quiet, smooth ride and quick acceleration.

In November, a terminal loop was opened at Hornusstrasse for routes 1 and 4, and the Komturplatz loop dismantled after only six years use, to make way for a traffic island.

Up until then, the trams had monopolised public transport in the central area, with buses providing feeder services only. This all changed on 6 December 1964,

when one of the bus routes was extended through Bertoldsbrunnen. This was followed by a second in 1966. Although this reduced the number of transfers passengers were obliged to make, the additional roadspace taken up by the buses only contributed to the congestion.

Five more GT4s, numbered 109-13, were delivered by Esslingen in the early months of 1966. These differed from the first batch in that they were specified for one-man operation, increasing their capacity to 40 seated and 131 standing passengers. Cars 103-8 were modified for one-man operation by Rastatt in 1966/7.

The delight of spring in the Black Forest is captured in this photograph of the picturesque Günterstal route. GT4 car 105 and trailer 2: are approaching the Wonnhalde stop from the south, 20/4/68. *(collection Kaufhold/Hettinge*

Yet another numbering system

On 13 September 1967, a new vehicle numbering system was introduced in which the motor cars were assigned fleet numbers by type; 2-axle and bogie cars in the range 1-100 and 4-axle articulated cars from 101-200. The *Verbandstyp* trailer cars 126-43 became 226-43, and works cars were renumbered from 401 upwards. As a consequence, three 4-axle trams were renumbered; Sputnik 100 became 103''', GT4 103'' became 109'''', and GT4 109''' became 114'''. Assigning re-used numbers to many of the newer cars unfortunately made things more complicated.

To replace the remaining prewar cars, two further batches of GT4s were ordered from Rastatt, as Esslingen had ceased building tramcars. Identical to the Esslingen cars, 115-8 were delivered in December 1967/January 1968 and 119-22 in December 1968/January 1969.

Most of the prewar cars were withdrawn and scrapped, but some were transferred to the works fleet. Several others were snapped up by various museums, and details of these are contained in the section on preserved cars. Car number 56 is the sole surviving maximum-traction car and is currently maintained in running order by the VAG.

In 1970, three *Verbandstyp* motor cars, 65/70/1, were declared surplus to requirements, even though still in their youth by Freiburg standards. They were transferred to the works fleet and renumbered 401-3. Two years later, following the entry into service of the first 8-axle cars, they were joined by 64/6/72/3, which were renumbered 404-7, leaving only seven of the type in service. Of these, 67/8 were withdrawn and scrapped in 1976; 62 suffered the same fate in 1977 as did 63 two years later. Car 66 was withdrawn in 1978 and converted to railgrinder 405'' three years later; 61 was withdrawn in 1979 and stored until transferred to the *Strassenbahn*

The GT4 cars provided the backbone of the fleet throughout the seventies. In this view, car 107 slows as it approaches the Johanneskirche stop, while operating a route 2 short working to Hornusstrasse, circa 1980. (collection Kaufhold/Hettinger)

Museum Schönau (SMS) in 1981. Number 74 remained in service until 1978 when it was converted to a party tram, a capacity in which it survived until 1996.

Bus replacement?

At the end of the 'sixties the future of the tramway hung in the balance as the Council began to seriously consider replacing the trams with buses. In 1969, it published "The General Transport Plan for Freiburg", the main thrust of which was a proposal to introduce fast, high-capacity vehicles between the city and the mushrooming western suburbs. Three alternatives were defined;

- Replacement of the trams by high-capacity buses on new routes.
- New high-speed, high-capacity, segregated tram routes combined with upgrading the existing tramway.
- A futuristic *Kabinen-Taxi* system linking the city centre with Landwasser.

(above) The cream and green livery of Freiburg's first GT8 car, number 201, gleams as it stands outside Urachstrasse depot prior to entering service, much to the curiosity of passers-by, 11/11/71. It would soon join "Sputnik" 102 (below), seen here in Komturstrasse while operating a route 4 service to Littenweiler. (collection Kaufhold/Hettinger)

Following the withdrawal of the Verbandstyp motor cars, the trailers were used to boost the capacity on GT4 operated services during busy periods. Here, "Rangierwagen" 406 shunts trailer 241 on to the back of a GT4 car outside Komturstrasse depot, during the last week of trailer operation, 26/6/81. (collection Kaufhold/Hettinger)

The bus option was favoured by the majority of members, but the determination of a pro-tram Councillor managed to defer the decision until full evaluations had been carried out on the other options. The cabin system, promoted by DEMAG, would have been more at home in a leisure park. Computer-controlled, it comprised multiple 3-seater cabins, suspended from concrete girder rails, similar in principle to the *Wuppertal Schwebebahn* but on a smaller scale. With only one route specified, its inherent operating problems, low passenger capacity, and unsightly concrete structures, the *Kabinen-Taxi* was quickly eliminated.

Eight-axle trams

Early in 1971, a Council delegation visited several transport undertakings around the country and returned convinced that an extended and upgraded tramway was the best solution for Freiburg. To assess the capabilities of high-capacity tramcars, four 8-axle, single-ended, double-articulated, GT8 type cars, were ordered from Duewag of Düsseldorf. Numbered 201-4 and painted in the standard cream livery, they arrived between November 1971 and January 1972.

At nearly 33 metres, they were then the longest 8-axle articulated trams in Germany and introduced several innovative features to production tramcars, further details of which are contained in chapter 10. A total of 294 passengers could be carried, 89 of them seated.

Freiburger Verkehrs AG

1 January 1973 was a major milestone in the evolution of public transport in Freiburg, when the bus and tram services operated by the transport department were reorganised. The new undertaking, *Freiburger Verkehrs AG* (VAG), was placed under the control of a municipally-owned group which also incorporated the city electricity and gas undertakings, an arrangement which is not unusual in Germany.

The VAG's first task was to implement the measures designed to tackle traffic congestion in the inner city. Kaiser-Joseph-Strasse would be converted into a pedestrian precinct with continued access by tram routes 1 and 2, and bus routes A, B and C. Displaced motor vehicles would be diverted to a new ring-road around the central area.

The reconstruction of this major thoroughfare began in November 1973. The old surface and pavements were torn up and replaced with a single-level of cobblestones across the full width of carriageway. The tram tracks were relocated to enable the mediæval *Bächle*, small streams running in unprotected gulleys, to be reinstated. Because of their hazardous nature, first-time visitors to the city should remain vigilant and familiarise themselves with the locations of these gulleys.

The opportunity was also taken to install connecting curves at Bertoldsbrunnen in anticipation of future route alterations, although it would be several years before service cars would use them. When the work was completed in 1980, a speed limit of 25 km/h was applied to the trams and buses. The project was judged a complete success and gradually extended to cover much of the *Altstadt*, including Salzstrasse and Bertoldstrasse on the east/west tram corridor.

The 1973 oil crisis provided the newly formed VAG with a golden opportunity to demonstrate its capabilities, as private motor vehicles were banned from public roads on Sundays and restricted on weekdays. Many extra trams and buses were run on reduced headways to cater for the huge increase in demand. The VAG received high praise for the efficient way in which it had handled the crisis and the ability of the 8-axle cars to move large loads quickly, was recognised as a major factor. It was a bouyant Council that soon after confirmed its decision to extend the tramway with new routes, built to the then, new *Stadtbahn* standards.

7. *Stadtbahn* to Landwasser ...

The first modern extension

The first line would leave the existing tramway near the Bertoldstrasse/Bismarckallee junction, and cross the main railway line and station platforms on a new viaduct. This would contain cycle tracks, footpaths and a covered, twin-platform tram station. Escalators and lifts would provide direct connection with the railway platforms below. The line would continue on central reservation through Betzenhausen to Paduaallee and from there over segregated, private-right-of-way to Landwasser.

Before construction could begin, however, the inhabitants of Stühlinger began a series of protests concerning the length and design of the viaduct, and this took several years to resolve. It was March 1978 before work finally commenced on the 322-metre structure which became known as *Bahnhofsbrücke*. Construction of a second viaduct, 219 metres long, at Wolfgang Hoffmann Platz and the installation of six signal-controlled level-crossings along Sundgauallee began soon after. Induction loops were installed between the rails to allow approaching trams to trigger the traffic-light change sequence in their favour.

Ten GT8 articulated tramcars were ordered for operation on the line and the first, number 205, arrived in the summer of 1981. Apart from twin headlights, a 2.3-metre wide body and a striking new livery incorporating the city's red and white colours, it was externally identical to the 1971 batch. Built by Duewag, it was fitted with BBC chopper-controlled electronic equipment and 4 x 150-kW motors. The remaining cars (206-14) were delivered over the following nine months and were classified GT8/C (Chopper) by the VAG. As construction of the *Stadtbahn* was still in progress, they entered service on route 4 (Hornusstrasse – Littenweiler), as this was the only route with turning circles at both termini.

With their entry into service, the last 2-axle *Verbandstyp* trailers were withdrawn on 3 July 1981. During their final years, they were used behind the *"Sputniks"* and

GT4s, and several were saved for preservation. The *"Sputniks"* were also withdrawn at this time and relegated for use on driver training duties.

A short extension was opened in October 1982, when 210 metres of single track was added at Günterstal to provide direct interchange with the *Schauinslandbahn* feeder bus service.

Trial running over *Bahnhofsbrücke* began in April 1983, and on 6 May a group of Councillors rode a section of the line in party tram 74, which was towed by diesel works car 407. The first 3.5 km of *Stadtbahn*, between Hbf and Paduaallee, was officially opened on Saturday, 9 December 1983, when decorated GT8 cars conveyed invited guests on the inaugural runs. This was probably the turning point in the history of Freiburg's tramway – the first new route for 55 years and more to follow. Travel on the line was free from 11.30 on the Saturday and all day on Sunday, when a full timetable was operated for an enthusiastic public.

On 11 December, the following tram route alterations were implemented:

1: **Littenweiler** – Bertoldsbrunnen – Hbf – **Paduaallee**

(Stadtbahn route served by GT8 cars on a 6-minute headway)

2: **Günterstal** – Bertoldsbrunnen – **Zähringen**

(Unchanged. Served by GT4 cars on a 12-minute headway)

3: **Hornusstrasse** – Bertoldsbrunnen – Hbf – **Hornusstrasse**

(Bidirectional circular route served by the *"Sputniks"* on a 12-minute headway)

4: **Hornusstrasse** – Bertoldsbrunnen – **Lorettostrasse**

(Peak-period, short working of route 2 served by GT4 cars on a 12-minute headway)

The sight of brand new GT8/C car 206 standing alongside 1901-built, 2-axle museum car 2, emphasises the advances made tramcar technology during the intervening 80 years, Komturstrasse depot, 03/08/81. The articulated car has a passenger capacity te times that of the little veteran.

(collection Kaufhold/Hettinge

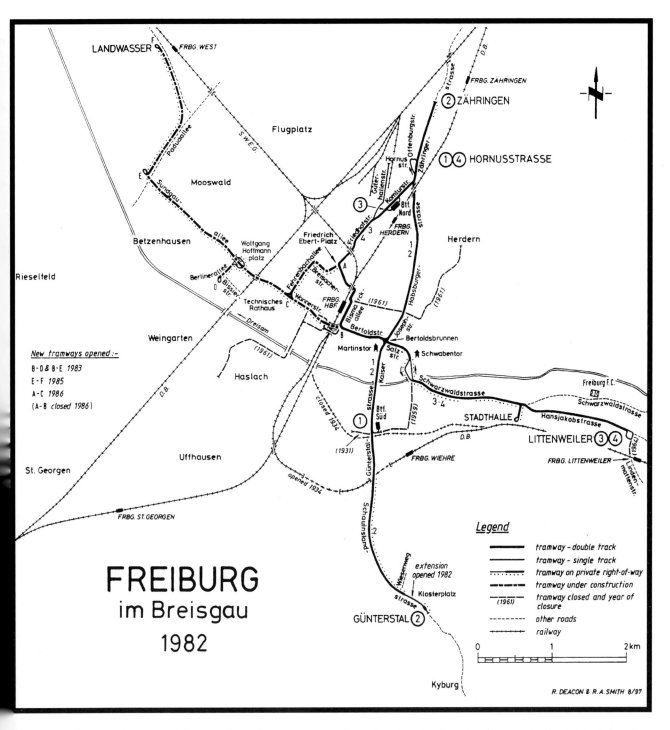

LANDWASSER F FRBG. WEST

Flugplatz

Padua allee

S.W.E.G.

Mooswald

Sundgau allee

Betzenhausen

Rieselfeld

Wolfgang Hoffmann platz

Berliner Allee

Bissier str.

Weingarten

Dreisam

Haslach

D.B.

St. Georgen

Uffhausen

FRBG. ST. GEORGEN

(2) ZÄHRINGEN
FRBG. ZÄHRINGEN

(1)(4) HORNUSSTRASSE

Hornus str.
Güter-hallenstr.
Komtur str.
Ottenburg str.
Zähringer-
strasse

(3)
Btf. Nord
FRBG. HERDERN

Herdern

Friedrich Ebert-Platz

Friedhofstr.

Habsburger.

(1961)

A

(1961)

Bismarck (1961)

FRBG. HBF

Technisches Rathaus

Brerzacher str.

Fehrenbachallee

Wannerstr.

C

B

Bertoldstr.

Joseph-str.

Bertoldsbrunnen

Martinstor
Salz-str.
Schwabentor

Schwarzwaldstrasse

Freiburg F.C.

Schwarzwaldstrasse

Hansjakobstrasse

STADTHALLE

3 4

LITTENWEILER (3)(4)

FRBG. LITTENWEILER

Lindenmattenstr.

(1961)

New tramways opened :-
B-D & B-E 1983
E-F 1985
A-C 1986
(A-B closed 1986)

(1961)

closed 1982

(1931)

opened 1934

(1)
Btf. Süd

Günterstal-str.
Schauinsland-str.

Kaiser

(1959)

FRBG. WIEHRE

D.B.

:2

extension opened 1982

Klosterplatz

Wiesenweg strasse

GÜNTERSTAL (2)

Kyburg

FREIBURG
im Breisgau
1982

Legend

tramway - double track
tramway - single track
tramway on private right-of-way
tramway under construction
(1961) tramway closed and year of closure
other roads
railway

0   1   2km

R. DEACON & R.A.SMITH 8/97

As the changes increased the number of passenger cars required for service, the *"Sputniks"* were reinstated on passenger duties.

The 2.2-km *Stadtbahn* section from Paduaallee to Landwasser was opened on 14 June 1985, when decorated GT8 cars 205, 206 and 210 carried invited guests to the opening ceremony at the new terminus. The line was built on concrete-sleepered track, over private-right-of-way, with intermediate stops at Moosgrund and *Diakonie Krankenhaus* (hospital). A large Park & Ride facility, partly enclosed by a turning loop and layover track, and a bus interchange was provided at the terminus, together with waiting room, toilets and a kiosk.

A short spur from the *Stadtbahn* was also opened on the same day. Branching off route 1 at the Runzmattenweg stop, it turned south alongside Berliner Allee

for a few hundred metres over private-right-of-way to a turning circle at Bissierstrasse. Although it was designed as a temporary facility, prior to the construction of a much longer extension, the terminus contained all the facilities found at other new termini. Its opening saw the reintroduction of a route numbered 5, running from Bissierstrasse, via Hbf and Bertoldsbrunnen to Zähringen, and operated by GT4 cars.

The final section of the first phase of *Stadtbahn* construction was opened on 28 September 1986, between Technisches Rathaus and Friedrich-Ebert-Platz, when routes 3 and 4 were diverted from Bismarckallee and Kreuz-strasse, over *Bahnhofsbrücke* to Technisches Rathaus. With four routes now using the viaduct, a frequent service was provided from the city centre to the railway station and the university complex on the western side of the city.

GT4 cars 104 on route 4 and 109 on route 3 in the standard cream and green livery of the era, layover at the Hornusstrasse terminus on19/4/84. Car 104 still has its couplers even though trailer operation had ceased three years earlier. *(F.van der Gragt)*

New route, new livery! GT4 car 117 shows off the city's red and white colours as it runs down the 6% ramp leading from Bahnhofs brücke to the Escholzstrasse stop in the background, while on its way to Bissierstrasse on route 5, 10/7/85. *(F. van der Grag*

The *Stadtbahn* cost DM 87 million to build, 60% of which came from national grants and 25% from the *Land* government of Baden-Württemberg. The steepest gradient was the 6% ramp on the approach to the west end of Bahnhofsbrücke and the tightest curve the 25-metre turning circle at Landwasser. Power was fed to the exten-

sion at 750 volts dc by 3 x 750 kVA and 2 x 1125 kV. transformers, and the power supplied to the remainde of the system was similarly increased. Speeds of up t 60 km/h are easily attainable on the Paduaallee – Land wasser section and average commercial speeds of 2 km/h have reduced the journey time from Landwasse

Two views of the opening of the Landwasser extension on 14/6/85. Garlanded GT8/C car 206 is seen leaving the Diakonie Kranken-haus stop (above), while sister car 205, driven by Mayor Böhme, arrives to an enthusiastic welcome at Landwasser (below).
(collection Kaufhold/Hettinger)

the city from 23 minutes on the displaced bus serv-e, to 14 minutes by tram.

The number of people using the *Stadtbahn* grew rap-ly and a shortage of trams began to cause serious vercrowding, especially during peak-hours. As there as no funding allocation for new cars, the VAG pur-ased eight second-hand GT4 cars from the *Stuttgarter trassenbahn AG*. Dating from 1964 and numbered 687/

93/700/2-6, they arrived in Freiburg in 1985/6, complete with Scharfenberg couplers to allow them to continue running in coupled pairs. A two-car unit could accom-modate 354 passengers, 96 of them seated. They were renumbered 151-8 and entered service on route 1 in their smart yellow, black and white livery.

Another two ex-Stuttgart GT4s, numbers 696 and 730, were purchased in 1988 and renumbered 160 and

A unique sight, at least in Freiburg, was captured in this photograph of three former Stuttgart GT4 cars, 152, 155 and 151, on a test run near Am Bischofskreuz, 10/10/85. The leading car (152) operated in its former all-yellow advertising livery for six weeks until its window surrounds were painted white. *(collection Kaufhold/Hettinger)*

159 respectively. Car 160 was painted all-over red with advertisements for the *Schauinsland* cable car, and was available for hire as a *Partywagen*.

By the end of 1989, the number of passengers using the trams had risen by 25% since opening of the *Stadtbahn*.

The red and white livery proved very popular and the first-series GT8s, the GT4s, *"Sputniks"* 101 and 103, and driver training car 401 were painted in the new livery as they passed through major overhaul.

Towards the end of 1988, a DM 30 million order was placed with Duewag for a further eleven 8-axle articulated trams with chopper electronic-control equipment from ABB. Externally similar to the 1981 batch of cars, they were easily distinguishable by the large windows in their low-floor (Niederflur) centre sections. Known as type GT8/N in Freiburg, the first car, number 221, arrived on 2 June 1990 and was joined by 222 shortly after. They entered service on route 1 where they were joined by the remainder over the next six months. These were the last high-floor "standard" cars to be built by Duewag.

Bismarckallee a few months before this section of track was closed in 1986, as seen from Bahnhofsbrücke. GT4 cars 109, 118 and 1 are operating on routes 3 and 4 outside the post-war Hauptbahnhof, on the left of the picture. *(collection Kaufhold/Hettinge*

The low-floor centre section is clearly visible in this view of GT8/N car 221 crossing the Rotteckring when working a route E Stadthalle - Paduaallee peak-hour duty. Behind it is sister car 231 operating a route 1 service to Landwasser, 4/92. (author)

Their arrival signalled the end for the ex-Stuttgart cars. Car 158 had been withdrawn and scrapped in Komturstrasse depot on 30 November 1988 following a major technical failure, and the same fate awaited the rest following their withdrawal in July 1990. Instead, all nine cars were donated to the city of Halle as part of Freiburg's contribution to the regeneration programme for the former East German republic. The cars left for Halle in October 1990.

The *"Sputniks"* meanwhile moved from their regular haunt on route 3 to route 5 for their final months in regular service, as they too were withdrawn before the year was out. They continued to be used as extras during the busy pre-Christmas shopping periods, and as football extras following the promotion of Freiburg to the first division of the *Bundesliga*. All three performed their final duties on route 5 on 11 December 1993.

The success of the football team attracts large crowds, and an intensive tram service is operated on match days. Up to thirteen "Football Extras" are held on the Stadthalle (also known as Möslestrasse) loop until shortly before the final whistle, when they run empty to the Littenweiler loop and back into Hansjakobstrasse to await the fans. A queue of trams 500 metres long is a common occurrence. The installation of a south-to-east connecting curve at Stadthalle in 1996 overcame the problem of reversing cars into Schwarzwaldstrasse, prior to their run to Littenweiler. An agreement between the football club and the VAG allows holders of match tickets to travel to the ground by tram at no additional cost.

Upgrading and more extensions

Freiburg's geographical position relative to the Black Forest, dictates that future expansion projects will be mainly concentrated to the south, west and north of the city. In the late eighties, a steering committee, composed of members of the VAG, the city and local authorities, carried out a study into future public transport require-

ments for the whole Freiburg region. This culminated in the publication of the *Gesamt Verkehrs Konzept* – GVK (Overall Transport Concept) in September 1990, in which proposals for the modernisation and expansion of the *Stadtbahn* over a ten to fifteen year period were outlined. New routes, extensions and traffic management schemes were assigned to one of two categories:

Phase 1 – Short Term

Construction of new routes and upgrading on existing routes.

New route:
- Johanneskirche to Am Lindenwäldle, via Carl-Kistner-Strasse.

Extensions:
- Bissierstrasse to Auf Der Haid, via Weingarten
- Littenweiler. Lassbergstrasse to Kappler Strasse, 1.5 km, using adjoining railway alignment for final 1 km.
- Zähringen. Reutebachgasse to Gundelfingen Süd, 1.5 km.
- Landwasser to Hochdorf.
- Am Lindenwäldle to Rieselfeld, 1.7 km.

Trambaan ([1]):
- Habsburger Strasse
- Zähringer Strasse
- Schwarzwaldstrasse
- Hansjakobstrasse
- Kaiser-Joseph-Strasse (southern end)

Phase 2 – Long Term

Routes where upgrading or construction would commence after the turn of the century.

Extensions:
- Weingarten to St Georgen-Friedhof.

A wet spring day, sees second-series GT8/C car 211 descending the Bahnhofsbrücke ramp and into Bertoldstrasse while working route 5 duty to Hornusstrasse. The Stühlinger Kirche, in the background, once provide the terminus for an earlier route 5, 4/92.
(author

- Weingarten to Merzhausen.
- Link to the airport.

Trambaan (¹):

- Günterstalstrasse

Priority was given to the Bissierstrasse – Auf der Haid extension as this would enable part of the tram fleet to be housed in Betriebshof West, thereby relieving the overcrowding in Komturstrasse, and facilitating the transfer of tramcar maintenance and overhaul from Urachstrasse. The projected cost of the new line, including rolling stock, was DM 122.5 million, 85% of which would come from *Land* and Federal grants. Construction of the 2.8-km extension began in 1991.

In January 1991, sixteen 8-axle, double-ended, GT8 type articulated cars were ordered from Duewag with electrical equipment from ABB, for operation on the Haid route. Classified by the VAG as GT8/Z (Zwei-Richtung), their specification featured, four sets of double doors on each side, a spacious interior with a 48% low floor area and four bogies, each incorporating 2 x 80-kW, water-cooled polyphase ac motors, a completely new feature for Freiburg.

Passenger capacity was quoted as 84 seated and 242 standing, assuming a crush load of 8/m², impressive figures for a vehicle 33 metres in length and 2.[?] metres wide.

To cater for the continual increase in passengers along the east-west corridor, a GT8-operated peak-hour short-working was introduced between Stadthalle and Paduaallee as route E on 25 November 1991. GT8 cars also took over some of the duties on route 5, but these had to turn short at Hornusstrasse as there was no turning circle at Zähringen. To compensate, GT4 cars operating anticlockwise on circular route 3 were extended from Hornusstrasse to Zähringen.

In the spring of 1992, the order for low-floor cars was increased to 26, following a decision to replace the GT[?] cars on the Zähringen – Günterstal service. Delivery [?] the first batch, 241-56, began on 23 September 199[?] and test running began with 241 between Wonnhald[?] and Wiesenweg on 4 October. It entered service on rou[?] 4 on 23 November 1993.

(¹) A *Trambaan* is a commonly accepted Dutch term describing a street tramway which is physically segregated from other road traff[?] Prime examples can be found in cities such as Amsterdam. In concept, the tracks are laid in a paved or surfaced section of carriagew[?] which is raised approximately 100 mm above the surface of the roadway on either side. The edges are usually canted to enable mo[?] vehicles to use them during emergencies.

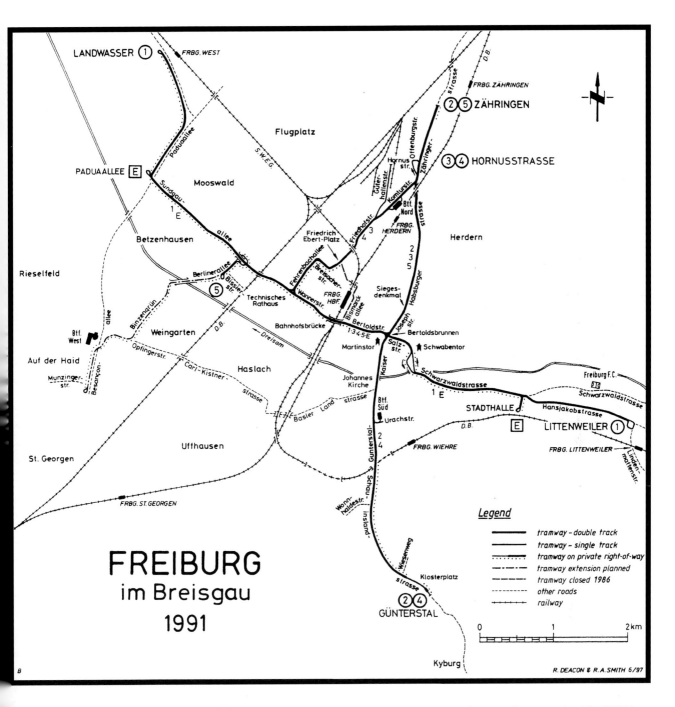

FREIBURG
im Breisgau
1991

Legend

▬▬▬	tramway – double track
───	tramway – single track
··········	tramway on private right-of-way
─ · ─ · ─	tramway extension planned
─ ·· ─ ·· ─	tramway closed 1986
- - - - -	other roads
┼┼┼┼┼	railway

0   1   2 km

R. DEACON & R.A. SMITH 6/97

(left) This busy scene was taken outside the Stadttheater and shows GT4 car 111 on its way to Günterstal on route 4, while GT8/N car 230 picks up passengers heading for Landwasser on route 1, 7/93. (right) The Hauptbahnhof tram stop is located directly above the station platforms and has direct escalator and lift connections. GT8/N car 224 is about to accelerate away for Landwasser on route 1, 7/93. *(author)*

On their last day in service, all three "Sputniks" operated route 5 duties between Bissierstrasse and Hornusstrasse. Two of them are seen here at the Hauptstrasse stop in Habsburger Strasse, 11/12/93. Car 103 was subsequently adapted for use as an advertising car and 102 languished in Komturstrasse for fifteen months before being scrapped. (S.Kirner

The permanent way gang step aside to allow GT8 car 204 to leave the Brauerei Ganter stop and run onto the central reservation Schwarzwaldstrasse, 8/94. (autho

(above) Two GT4 cars 106 and 108 pass at Bertoldsbrunnen while working on route 4, shortly before their departure for Halberstadt, 8/94. (below) For their final months of regular service in Freiburg, the GT4 cars shared duties with GT8/Z cars on route 4. Here we see GT4 car 117 turning into Bertoldstrasse while GT8/Z car 246 "Zähringen" picks up passengers heading for Günterstal, 8/94. Car 117 was sold to Brandenburg in 1997. (author)

8. ... Auf der Haid and Rieselfeld

The Haid extension was officially opened at 11.30 on Saturday, 26 March 1994, with ceremonies at Munzinger Strasse, Binzengrün and Zähringen. Three decorated GT8/Z cars, 243, 246 and 247, were used to carry the invited guests and, in recognition of the event, each car was given a name; 243 – 'Zähringen', 246 – 'Weingarten' and 247 – 'St Georgen'. For the remainder of the day and all day Sunday, the citizens of Freiburg enjoyed free access to the entire VAG network.

New schedules introduced on the Sunday, saw the tram system simplified from five routes to three, routes 2 and 3 being withdrawn during the afternoon of 24 March. GT4 car 116, with only five passengers on board, was the last to operate on route 2, departing from Günterstal at 14.07. The route's demise brought an end to a long chapter in the history of Freiburg's trams, as route 2 had operated virtually unchanged since the opening of the system 93 years earlier.

The system now comprised three routes:

1: **Littenweiler** – Messplatz – Bertoldsbrunnen – Hbf – Paduaallee – **Landwasser**

4: **Hornusstrasse** – Friedrich-Ebert-Platz – Hbf – Bertoldsbrunnen – **Günterstal**

5: **Zähringen** – Siegesdenkmal – Bertoldsbrunnen – Hbf – Bissierstrasse – **Munzinger Strasse.**

A 7.5-minute service was introduced on routes 1 and 5, and a 10-minute service on route 4 between 06.45 and 18.45, with extra cars operated during rush-hours. Route 1 remained the domain of GT8/8C cars 201-14 and GT8/N cars 221-31, while routes 4 and 5 became the province of GT8/Z cars 241-66.

When delivery of the first series of GT8/Z cars was completed, seven GT4 cars – 110-2/4/9-22 – were sold to Nordhausen, primarily for use on the Ilfeld section of the *Harzquerbahn*, which had been authorised for electrification. Car 114 was fitted with a diesel generator for trial running, but conversion of the line for electric operation has not so far materialised. Some of the other cars entered service on the town's tramway bearing their ex-Freiburg fleet numbers, although cars 110-2/4 were recently renumbered 91-4 and repainted yellow and white.

Five more GT4 cars were disposed of as delivery of the second batch of GT8/Z cars got under way in July 1994. Cars 105/6/8/13/5 were sold to Halberstadt, where they were renumbered 161/4/5/2/3 respectively.

During 1995, car 121 was painted blue and converted to a *Partywagen* as a replacement for 74, and car 109 was reclassified as a VAG museum car.

As for the *"Sputniks"*, 101 was scrapped in 1995 following a motor failure, 102 was suddenly scrapped in 1996, having been prospective candidate for preservation, and 103 was panelled over, painted green and renumbered 100 (its original number) to become an advertising car in September 1994.

With the introduction of the winter timetable on 29 September 1996, the three bus services operating through Bertoldsbrunnen, routes 10, 11, and 12, were

Following the demise of the GT4 cars, route 4 became wholly GT8/Z operated. Here we see "advertising" car 265 accelerating awa from Martinstor and the pedestrianised zone while working a service to Günterstal, 9/96. The fast food restaurant located under th. archway offers quick sustenance for those with little time to spare.
(autho

GT8/Z car 263, also in advertising livery, is about to pass beneath the railway bridge at Okenstrasse while en route to Zähringen, 28/5/96. The bridge was rebuilt in 1920 to allow the trams to reach this outlying village. (F. van der Gragt)

he first of the new generation cars for Freiburg, GT8/Z car 241 stops at Maria-von-Rudloff-Platz during the first weekend of service on route It retains its attractive light-blue livery depicting the Schauinslandbahn, complete with a cable car image at each doorway, 14/09/97 .
(collection Kaufhold)

All the tram routes are now operated by high capacity 8-axle cars as depicted on this and the next page. GT8/N cars 226 and 229 pass at the route 1 stop in the narrow confines of Oberlinden, 7/97. (author)

diverted away from Kaiser-Joseph-Strasse and on to the Rotteckring ring road, leaving the trams as the sole public transport provider in the pedestrianised zone. However, following complaints from passengers, bus route 10 was restored to its old route via Bertolds-brunnen.

The remaining GT4 cars (104/7/16-8) were kept in reserve and, after a period of relative inactivity, saw short periods of service during the latter part of 1996, when they were used to release GT8/Z cars from route 4 for duties as football extras. On Saturdays during advent, they were also used on a special service operating from Wonnhalde to Hornusstrasse via Bertoldsbrunnen and Siegesdenkmal, along part of the old route 2. But, as their butterfly type doors were unable to clear the slightly higher platforms at new and refurbished stops, they spent most of their time in Komturstrasse depot.

Work on installing the first section of track for the re-extension to Littenweiler Bahnhof and construction of the extension to Rieselfeld began in the spring of 1996. As work on the Rieselfeld branch neared completion, construction engineers moved south to the Günterstal route, to begin the complete renewal of track and over-

head on the segregated section between Holbeinstrasse and Wiesenweg. As a consequence, route 4 was cut back to Lorettostrasse for six months from 23 March while the reconstruction proceeded.

The final clearout of redundant GT4 cars took place in the autumn of 1997 when car 104 was sold to Halberstadt where it was renumbered 166, and cars 116-8 were sold to Brandenburg, leaving car 107 pending disposal.

The Rieselfeld extension was opened in traditional festive style at 14.00 on 13 September, 1997, using museum motor car 56 and *Verbandstyp* trailer 142, the latter on its first outing, and GT8/Z cars 243, 245 and 254, each wearing a garland of flowers and carrying invited guests. The procession of cars departed from Bissierstrasse and headed for Rieselfeld where, a special ceremony was held at the Maria von Rudloff Platz stop, named after a well-known local doctor and town councillor. Car 254 was officially named *"Rieselfeld"* and the unveiling of a plaque was followed by speeches from the mayor, VAG chairman and other dignitaries. During the remainder of the afternoon and all day Sunday, the museum cars were operated between Rieselfeld and Hornusstrasse for the benefit of the public.

(above)GT8/Z cars 254 on route 4 and (below) 259 on route 5, demonstrate their ability to operate safely in the busy pedestrianised centre of the city. Bertoldsbrunnen, 7/97.   (author)

9. The routes

The current routes

At the beginning of 1994, six tram routes, 1 to 5 plus peak-hour route E were operating, but with the opening of the Haid extension on 26 March that year, routes 2, 3 and E were withdrawn and the headways increased on the other routes.

At the time of writing, the tramway system comprises routes 1, 4, 5 and 6 totalling 24.3 km in length, operated by a fleet of 51 eight-axle tramcars.

Route colours began appearing on destination blinds following the introduction of the GT8/C cars, the colour forming the background to a white route number. This chapter describes each route as viewed from the perspective of the driver.

Route 1: (Red)

Littenweiler – Landwasser

The eastern terminus of route 1 is in the suburb of Littenweiler and comprises a double-track loop, passenger shelters, toilets, crew accommodation and kiosk. It is also the terminus and interchange with several feeder bus routes. The trackwork was recently relaid and includes the first section for the extension to Kappler Strasse.

The early morning sun catches GT8/N car 225 preparing to depart from Littenweiler on a route 1 service to Landwasser, having picked-up passengers from feeder-bus 42. GT8/C car 209 in the background awaits its turn to draw forward. A waiting room, toilets and kiosk are out of sight on the left. *(author)*

On leaving the terminus, our tram enters Hansjakobstrasse, a long, broad suburban road with elegant, mid-'thirties, detached houses on either side. The tracks are located in the centre of the road and demarcated from other traffic by white lines. Three traditional style pavement stops are encountered along this thoroughfare, each protected by traffic lights. Approaching trams trigger the change sequence, forcing following motor vehicles to stop and wait while passengers board or alight.

At Schiff our car swings left on to a reservation in the centre of Schwarzwaldstrasse, the B31 main access road into the Black Forest, and crosses the trailing points for cars leaving the Stadthalle turning loop. This is used for football specials and events held at the large exhibition hall and show ground in *Messplatz*. Apart from a short on-street section, the tramway is fully segregated, partly on *trambaan* and partly on sleepered vignoles type track. Five stops are encountered between here and Schwabentorbrücke, each with shelters, low-height platforms and railings, and reached by light-controlled crossings.

Schwarzwaldstrasse at Stadthalle, looking east towards the Schiff Gasthaus, which can be seen between the distant trees. GT8/N car 224 has no trouble passing the slow moving traffic as it accelerates along the centrally located trambaan towards the city.

(author)

At Schwabentorbrücke, the tracks follow separate paths on one-way streets and, after crossing the river Dreisam, our car enters a short section of *trambaan* as it approaches the imposing *Schwabentor* gate tower ahead. We cross the busy Schlossbergring, the castle grounds and forest rising high on the right, and pass through the right hand archway into the serenity of Oberlinden.

The streets are now cobbled and the first *Bächle* emerges from under the roadway opposite the famous *Rote Bären* Inn. Many traditional, prewar style buildings are found in this area, which is reserved for use by pedestrians, cyclists and trams. The speed limit in the pedestrianised area is 25 km/h. We continue at a leisurely pace through the narrow Salzstrasse to the crossroads at Bertoldsbrunnen, where many passengers alight. Then, cautiously edging our way over the

The Schwabentor overshadows GT8/N car 227 as it emerges fro the archway, which was cut through the ground floor of the adjoining house in 1913 to provide better access for trams approachi the city from the east. *(auth*

This replica "tramwagen", recently constructed by the Verein Original Tram Basel, is identical to the vehicles Adolf Jenne purchased from Basel in 1896. It is seen here at Holzmarkt with GT8/Z car 249 in the background, while on a short-term loan to Freiburg, 4/7/95. (Stefan Kirner)

The oldest VAG preserved trams are shown together in this view of maximum traction car 56 of 1927 and two-axle car 2 dating from 1901 as they approach Weisenweg while on route to Günterstal 25/5/79. (collection Kaufhold)

Converted from Verbandstyp car 65 in 1970, driver training car 401 is caught on camera by the old university complex in Bertoldstrasse, while on a training session in its new red and white livery, 6/4/88. *(collection Kaufhold)*

Built as Verbandstyp passenger cars 64 and 72, works cars 404 and 406 were adapted for depot shunting in the early 'seventies. They are seen entering Urachstrasse in their bright orange livery, 12/93. *(Stefan Kirner)*

"The Clockwork Lemon"! Verbandstyp motor car 74 stands in the confines of Komturstrasse depot shortly before taking a party of visitors for a tour of the city, 9/89. (author)

The quiet hum of a GT4 car's motors can still be heard in Freiburg, following the conversion of car 121 to a party tram in 1995. Painted in the attractive livery of its sponsor, it waits to pick up passengers at the Bollenstaudenstrasse stop in Reiselfeld during the first weekend of operation on route 6, 14/9/97. (collection Kaufhold)

"Sputnik" 101 on the reservation in Fehrenbachallee, shows off its newly applied red and white livery while operating a circular route 3 service, 22/9/87. (collection Kaufhold)

Resplendent in its new red and white livery, "Sputnik" 103 arrives at Hauptbahnhof as GT8 car 205 prepares to depart for Landwasser, with the Stühlinger Kirche in the background, 6/86. (author)

"All three "Sputniks" were captured in this photograph which was taken in Halle II, Btf Nord, five months before their withdrawal from regular passenger service, 16/7/90.
(Stefan Kirner)

During their final years the Sputniks were mainly used for driver training or, as on this occasion, as football extras. Here they wait on the Stadthalle loop for the homeward bound fans on the last day they were used on football duties, 11/9/93.
(collection Kaufhold)

Ex-Stuttgart GT4 cars 151 and 155 were caught in Hansjakobstrasse during their first test run in Freiburg. They retained their attractive yellow and white livery until they were sold to Halle five years later, 14/9/85.   *(collection Kaufhold)*

GT4 car 160 ran in Freiburg for one year only, during which time it sported this all-red livery portraying the delights of the Schauinsland cable car. It is seen arriving at Stadthalle with car 159, while bound for Littenweiler on the last day of service of the ex-Stuttgart cars, 13/7/90   *(collection Kaufhold)*

Günterstal village centre is the location for this October 1987 view of GT4 car 106 on route 2 about to depart for Zähringen via the city centre. *(author)*

GT4 car 118 passes the old university building in Bertoldstrasse as it accelerates slowly away from the Bertoldsbrunnen stop while working a route 4 duty to Hornusstrasse, 9/89. *(author)*

Two views of GT4 car 121 on route 2; above, it is seen waiting for cars operating on other routes to arrive at Bertoldsbrunnen on a quiet Sunday afternoon, 6/88, while below, it speeds through the most scenic part of the system, the section between Wonnhalde and Günterstal, 9/89. *(author)*

Still in immaculate condition, GT4 cars 109 and 118 stand in Halle II, Btf Nord, six months after their withdrawal from regular service. The VAG subsequently designated car 109 as a museum car and intend to eventually return it to its original cream livery and number, 103. Car 118 was sold to Brandenburg in 1997. 18/6/95.   *(collection Kaufhold)*

First-generation GT8 car 202 was operating as a driver training car (Fahrschulwagen) when this view was captured outside Komturstrasse depot, 9/96.   *(author)*

Second-generation GT8/C car 209 speeds along the grass-covered trambaan in Sundgauallee while operating a route 1 service to Littenweiler, 9/94. *(author)*

GT8/C car 210 on route 1 and GT4 car 117 on route 3 are seen outside the Stadttheater during the period of the 1986 Landesgarten show, which was held in Betzenhausen. *(author)*

The third-generation of GT8 cars can be distinguished from their predecessors by their low-floor centre sections. Here, GT8/N car 222 is overshadowed by the tall spire of the Münster as it works a route 1 service to Littenweiler, Oberlinden, 9/96.

(author)

GT8/N car 225 comes to a stop at Runzmattenweg while on route for Landwasser. Cars from this batch (221 - 231) are rostered on every third duty as a minimum, to ensure that the VAG fulfils its customer guarantee of a regular service of low-floor vehicles on route 1. Every duty on the route will be operated by low-floor cars once the "Combinos" enter service. 9/96.

(author)

Until the new facilities were opened at Betriebshof West in 1994, several GT8 cars were stabled overnight in the open works yard at the back of Komturstrasse depot. Here we see cars 207 and 230 in the yard, having finished their duties for the day, 22/4/95. (author)

Until 1991, new trams were delivered to the Güterbahnhof by rail and towed through the former permanent-way yard, then along Kaiserstuhlstrasse and on to Urachstrasse depot. Commencing with the GT8/Z cars, low-loading trailers delivered the cars directly to Komturstrasse depot by road. The photograph shows car 243 shortly after its arrival, 18/11/93. (Stefan Kirner)

A brand new car on a brand new line! GT8/Z car 257 on route 5 crosses the river Dreisam and B31 autobahn while on its way to Munzinger Strasse during its first week of service, 8/94.   *(author)*

The trambaan alongside Besançonallee is the location for this view of GT8/Z car 257 on route 5, with the Munzinger Strasse terminus, St Georgen Kirche and vineclad hills of the Black Forest in the background, 8/94.   *(author)*

What better way to get your message across. The environmentally-friendly VAG slogan borne by GT8/Z car 242, states that it can carry up to 326 passengers while occupying the same amount of roadspace as six motor cars which on average, carry a total of only ten people. The car was photographed on the trambaan which runs the length of Binzengrün, Weingarten. 8/94.
(author)

GT8/Z car 250, which was the second car to enter service in an all-over advertising livery, is seen on a route 5 service on the grass-covered Besançonallee trambaan, 8/94.
(author)

All-over advertising is now a common sight on Freiburg's trams, and some interesting designs have appeared. A prime example is GT8/Z car 256, which is advertising one of the city's bakeries. Covered in buns and with appropriately positioned "oven" doors, it was captured on the trambaan in Breisacherstrasse while operating a route 4 service to Hornusstrasse, 9/96.
(author)

GT8/Z car 257 has carried several advertising liveries since entering service. This blue and yellow example contrasts well with the lush green vegetation on the Fehrenbachallee trambaan. Robert-Koch-Strasse, 9/96. *(author)*

The Schauinslandbahn as it was then. Car 6, built in 1930, arrives back at the lower terminus on the last day of operation before work started on the complete rebuild of the line, Friedrichshof, 11/10/87.　　　　　　　*(collection Kaufhold)*

The Schauinslandbahn is it is now. New, smaller cabins afford magnificent views of the Black Forest, Freiburg and, on a clear day, the Vosges mountains of France beyond, 15/8/89.　　　　　　　*(collection Kaufhold)*

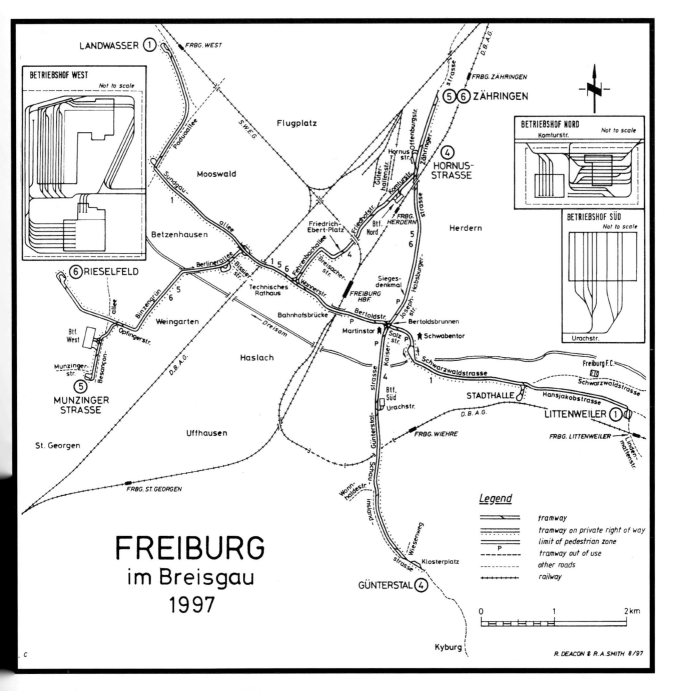

BETRIEBSHOF WEST
Not to scale

BETRIEBSHOF NORD
Komturstr. *Not to scale*

BETRIEBSHOF SÜD
Not to scale
Urachstr.

LANDWASSER ① FRBG. WEST

FRBG. ZÄHRINGEN
⑤⑥ ZÄHRINGEN

Flugplatz

Mooswald

④ HORNUS-
STRASSE

Herdern

⑥ RIESELFELD

Betzenhausen

Weingarten

Haslach

Ufthausen

St. Georgen

⑤ MUNZINGER
STRASSE

Friedrich-
Ebert-Platz

Technisches
Rathaus

Bahnhofsbrücke

FREIBURG
HBF.

Bertoldstr.

Martinstor

Siegesdenkmal

Bertoldsbrunnen

Schwabentor

Freiburg F.C.

Schwarzwaldstrasse

STADTHALLE

Hansjakobstrasse

LITTENWEILER ①

FRBG. LITTENWEILER

Btf.
Süd
Urachstr.

FRBG. WIEHRE

Klosterplatz

FRBG. ST. GEORGEN

FREIBURG
im Breisgau
1997

GÜNTERSTAL ④

Kyburg

Legend

———	tramway
┅┅┅	tramway on private right of way
——P——	limit of pedestrian zone
- - -	tramway out of use
- - - -	other roads
+++++	railway

0   1   2 km

R. DEACON & R.A. SMITH 8/97

Having discharged its complement of passengers by the VAG "Pluspunkt" information centre, GT8/N 222 moves cautiously forward as passengers from GT8/C car 214 wait to cross behind it. (author)

half "grand union", we come to a halt at the Bertold-strasse stop.

This is the city centre and main shopping area, and is alive with people going in all directions, oblivious of the passing trams. Bertoldsbrunnen is the hub of the tramway system with easy interchange between the four tram routes and bus route 10. A VAG information centre, called *"Pluspunkt"* was opened at Salzgasse 3 in July 1996 to replace the well-concealed original ticket office on the opposite side of the junction.

All four tram routes now share the tracks as we continue along Bertoldstrasse and cross the Rotteckring to the next stop outside the Stadttheater. On leaving Bertoldstrasse, our tram climbs the ramp leading to the covered interchange on *Bahnhofsbrücke*. Footpaths and cycle paths flank both sides of this impressive structure. The twin spires of the *Stühlinger Kirche* stand proud ahead while, down below, the broad expanse of the main line railway tracks fans out. Escalators and lifts provide direct connections to the station platforms and main ticket office.

First series GT8 car 203 arrives at the Technisches Rathaus stop serving the large university complex located here, on route to Littenweiler. Note the car's large twin headlights which were fitted during its last major overhaul. The connecting curve in the foreground is used for non-scheduled workings, mainly between the Komturstrasse and Besançonallee depots. (author)

On leaving the station we gather speed down the 6% exit ramp, twisting right and then left as we approach the Escholzstrasse stop. This is located by a busy, light-controlled junction with predominantly prewar shops and apartment buildings. On crossing the road we enter Wannerstrasse on a grass-covered central reservation, for a short run to the next junction at Technisches Rathaus, where the tracks for route 4 branch right into Fehrenbachallee. A second pair of connecting curves is used for depot workings only. The large university faculty located here supplies a constant stream of students as tram passengers.

The line continues on grass-covered tree-lined, private-right-of-way, to Runzmattenweg, where routes 5 and 6 branch off to the right and down a ramp. We continue on, across the busy Wolfgang-Hoffmann-Platz on a tram-only viaduct, and sweep down to a grass-covered, central reservation in Sundgauallee. This is Betzenhausen, a modern suburb consisting primarily of low-rise apartment blocks. The ivy-clad overhead masts blend well with the abundance of greenery. Two tram stops with light-controlled access are passed as we head for Paduaallee, the terminus of route 1 from 1983 to 1985 and which has retained its turning loop for emergency use and short workings. Park & Ride facilities are located across the road and a kiosk and toilets are pro-

GT8/N car 223 runs on to the turning loop at Landwasser having deposited its passengers at the stop just behind it. The waiting room, kiosk, feeder-bus terminal and a large park & ride are to the right of the picture. Tram route 1 currently accounts for one-third of the total number of passengers carried on all VAG services. (author)

vided at the stop. Cross-city bus route 10 and several feeder bus routes terminate here.

The final leg of the journey passes through picturesque woodland, on private-right-of-way and roadside reservation, to the Landwasser terminus. Two intermediate stops, providing access to a hospital and residential property, comprise low platforms and passenger shelters. The terminal loop encircles a large Park & Ride facility, and incorporates a kiosk, toilets and bus interchange.

Route 1 is operated by single-ended GT8/8C type cars 201-14 and GT8/N cars 221-31. An extension is proposed to Löwen (Kappler Strasse), east of Littenweiler.

Although GT4 car 104 or route 2 no longer serve Günterstal, this photograph depicts the terminus, which is also used by feeder bus route 21, as it is today. The line was extended to this point in 1982 to provide better passenger interchange between the two transport modes. The small building houses a waiting room, crew room and toilets. (author)

Route 4: (Green)
Günterstal – Hornusstrasse

The picturesque village of Günterstal lies in a serene valley on the edge of the Black Forest on the southern outskirts of the city, and has been served by trams since 1901. The stub-end terminus is located at Dorfstrasse and is, at the time of writing, the most southerly tram terminus in Germany. Its crew facilities are shared with drivers from feeder bus route 21, which operates to the Schauinsland cable car line and villages beyond. Until 26 March 1994 the line was served by routes 2 and 4, but is now operated by cars on route 4 only.

We leave the terminus via a passing loop, and enter a short section of segregated single track leading to a second loop, and stop in Klosterplatz, the heart of the village. Our view to the left is dominated by the monastery and a neat row of period houses and shops, set back from the road, forming an attractive square on the right. As we pull away we pass through a narrow, single track archway under the former police station and into Schauinslandstrasse. A short burst of speed on segregated, double track brings us swiftly to the Wiesenweg stop.

From here, we accelerate away and begin a fast run beside the tree-lined Schauinslandstrasse, over private right-of-way, on one of the most picturesque sections on the system. Open fields rise gently towards the forest, which fans outwards and upwards as far as the eye can see. A kilometre or so later and we are slowing for the stop at Wonnhalde. This consists of low-level platforms and a large, rather drab, concrete passenger shelter. Passenger access is via a light-controlled cross

GT8/Z car 255 runs through the picturesque Black Forest as it approaches Wonnhalde. This section of track, which the VAG favours for its rolling stock photographs, was completely relaid and new overhead installed during the summer of 1997. *(author)*

Having taken its passengers on board, GT8/Z car 254 pulls away from the Bertoldsbrunnen stop in Bertoldstrasse for a run to Zähringen. Notice how far the points for cars heading in the opposite direction are located from the junction. *(author)*

ing. With little housing in the vicinity, it is a favourite spot for walkers attracted by the trails which lead off through the woods in all directions.

Our car pulls away, across the inbound carriageway of Schauinslandstrasse, and continues on private-right-of-way to the last of the segregated stops at Holbeinstrasse. Large period houses signal the beginning of the affluent Loretto district. From here the trams share the roadway with other vehicles, with gutter running as far as the crossroads and island stop at Lorettostrasse. On approaching the junction, we swing to the centre of the road, and the trailing points leading to Urachstrasse depot converge from the right.

A variety of small shops and residential properties borders both sides of the street, which leads to the island stop at Johanneskirche. Its tall spires overshadow the long platforms, which are also used by buses on route 10. Shelters and railings are provided for passenger protection.

GT4 car 122 was the last of these handsome vehicles to be built and is seen crossing the flag-bedecked Kaiserbrücke on route to Hornusstrasse. Ahead lies the Kaiser-Joseph-Strasse and the impressive Martinstor gateway. *(author)*

On pulling away, our driver carefully crosses the B31 carriageways and the river Dreisam on the Kaiserbrücke, as we head into Kaiser-Joseph-Strasse and the Holzmarkt tramstop. Located in the centre of the road, its basic construction consists of unprotected platforms and stop signs. The buildings in this part of the city are distinctly turn-of-the-century, and escaped most of the bombing.

The transition to cobbled road surfaces and the sight of the impressive *Martinstor* gate-tower looming up ahead, indicate that we are entering the pedestrianised

zone. Our tram passes through the right hand archway and slows to a crawl as it approaches the Bertoldsbrunnen crossroads. The statue and fountain in the centre were erected in 1964 to replace the original destroyed in the bombing. Ahead lies the main shopping area of Kaiser-Joseph-Strasse. After stopping briefly to let alighting passengers off, we move off and turn left into Bertoldstrasse and pull up at the boarding stop shared with routes 1, 5 and 6.

The Technisches Rathaus junction is the location for this view of GT8/Z car 243 on route 5, waiting for sister car 248 to complete its turn from Fehrenbachallee into Wannerstrasse while operating a route 4 duty to Günterstal. *(author)*

From here we share the same tracks as far as Technisches Rathaus, and turn north into Fehrenbachallee, a section of *Stadtbahn* opened in 1986. The tracks are located on grass-covered, tree-lined, private-right-of-way to the next stop at Robert-Koch-Strasse, where standard platforms and shelters are provided. A sharp right turn into Breisachstrasse, followed by a left into Hohenzollernstrasse, still on reserved track, brings us to the busy junction and stop at Friedrich-Ebert-Platz. Until 1986, routes 3 and 4 used a more direct but more congested route via Bismarckallee to reach this point.

We cross the junction and enter a short reservation, then swing into the centre of the road, before dipping under a low railway arch and up the other side to a stop at the main cemetery (*Hauptfriedhof*). The tracks continue to occupy the centre of the road for a short distance, then swing right into a segregated stop at Rennweg. The single track without overhead, which can be seen branching away to our left, leads to *Güterbahnhof*. It was used for the delivery of new trams until 1990, but sees little use now they are delivered by road.

One of several advertising cars on the system, GT8/Z car 265 carries the brightly coloured graphics for a city bookshop. It is seen in Zähringer Strasse shortly after leaving the Hornusstrasse terminus which is located by the tall apartment block in the distance. *(author)*

Our car accelerates away into Komturstrasse, with its low-rise prewar apartment blocks, and the depot can be seen just beyond the next stop at Eichstetter Strasse. The track layout in the depot affords some interesting shunting manoeuvres. No protection is given to the tracks in this quiet street, which leads to a large roundabout and tram stop in Komturplatz. For the final leg of the journey, we briefly join the tracks of route 5 in Zähringer Strasse, before turning left into Offenburger Strasse for a short run to the double-track terminus at Hornusstrasse, which is shared with bus routes 15 and 16. Passenger facilities here include toilets, shelter and kiosk.

Route 4 is currently operated by double-ended GT8/Z type cars 241-66.

Another advertising car, GT8/Z number 248 on this occasion, is seen laying over in the stub-end terminus of route 5 at Zähringen. At the scheduled time, it will move forward to pick up passengers waiting at the stop. *(author)*

Route 5: (Blue)

Zähringen – Munzinger Strasse

The Zähringen terminus of route 5 is currently the most northerly point on the tram system and is located in the centre of a small village-like street. One of the two platforms provided is used for boarding and the other for alighting. Terminating trams continue on to a short, single-track stub. Plans for an extension northwards to Gundelfingen have been published, although no date is scheduled for its construction.

On leaving the terminus, our tram runs on *trambaan* down the centre of Zähringer Strasse, the main approach road from the north, to the first stop at Tullastrasse, and then on tarmac-covered roadway to Hornusstrasse.

Both stops comprise platforms, shelters, protective railings and light-controlled crossings. At Hornusstrasse, the route 4 terminus can be seen on the right. Cars from

Siegesdenkmal, when the GT4 cars were still operating on route 5, sees GT4 car 110 picking up passengers at the newly constructed interchange, while en-route to Zähringen. The cable-car sign on the shelter, was to indicate that passengers wishing to ride the Schauinslandbahn should catch a tram here. *(author)*

this route share our tracks for a short run to Komturplatz, where they turn right into Komturstrasse. Cars on routes 5 and 6 continue across the junction and swing sharply left, under the cramped confines of a railway bridge, and then right to the first of three stops in Habsburger Strasse. This is a long and busy suburban road, lined with a variety of pre-war shops and residential accommodation. The tracks are located in the middle of the road and protected by white lines, but plans are afoot for the installation of a full *trambaan*.

At Siegesdenkmal, the tram stop forms an artificial island in the centre of the ring road, with passenger access by subways and light-controlled crossings. It also marks the northern boundary of the pedestrianised zone. We continue into Kaiser-Joseph-Strasse, running slowly past the bustling shoppers, to Bertoldsbrunnen and turn right to the tram stop in Bertoldstrasse. From here, cars on routes 5 and 6 share the tracks with routes 1 and 4 as far as Technisches Rathaus and with route 1 as far as Runzmattenweg.

At Runzmattenweg, we branch off to the right, down a single-track ramp and turn left under the route 1 viaduct to rejoin the inbound track on private-right-of way for a short run to Bissierstrasse. The area comprises mainly modern, medium-rise apartment buildings.

At Runzmattenweg, route 5's tracks diverge either side of the ramp leading to the Wolfgang-Hoffmann-Platz viaduct used by cars on route 1. GT8/Z car 255 is seen on route to Munzinger Strasse. Note how ivy is used to camouflage the concrete overhead mast. *(author)*

GT8/Z car 250 sports a smart grey advertising livery as it arrives at Bissierstrasse on a warm summer day. The track to the right of the tram forms part of the loop which was route 5's terminus until 1994. *(author)*

The view from the VAG Zentrum stop looking towards Munzinger Strasse as GT8/Z car 256 quietly speeds along the grass covered tracks. Trams will one day reach St Georgen church, the spire of which can just be seen in front of the vineclad hills in the background. *(author)*

Bissierstrasse was opened as an intermediate terminus for route 5 in 1986 and retains its Park & Ride facilities, passenger shelters, toilets, kiosk and terminal loop.

We now enter the 2.8-km extension which was opened on 26 March 1994. Tree-lined and fully landscaped to integrate with the immediate surroundings, the tracks are laid in a grass-covered, private-right-of-way throughout, affording a smooth and silent ride. After a short run alongside Berliner Allee, we cross the B31 and river on the Dreisambrücke, a purpose-built tram/cycle/pedestrian viaduct, and descend a 6% ramp into Binzengrün. Until the advent of the *Stadtbahn*, this was a broad suburban boulevard, served by five bus routes, but is now a more environmentally friendly, narrow two-lane road with a 30 km/h speed limit. The bus services were cut back to Munzinger Strasse or diverted when the tramway opened.

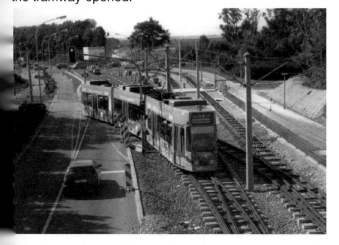

GT8/Z car 266 crosses Opfinger Strasse under traffic light control onto the newly laid junction for route 6. Land clearance for the new suburb of Rieselfeld is in progress to the right of the large hoarding in the background. *(author)*

The area is modern and pleasantly laid out with low-rise apartment blocks and housing. Two more stops are passed before reaching the junction at Opfinger Strasse, where we turn sharply right and stop at Am Lindenwäldle. The line continues for a short distance and passes under a footbridge before swinging left across Opfinger Strasse under traffic light control. The recently-opened tracks for route 6 to Rieselfeld can be seen to the right, but we head south through a short cutting to run along the east side of Besançonallee.

After a few hundred metres, our tram turns right, cross the dual-carriageway and access tracks to

Betriebshof West, to the penultimate stop outside the VAG head office, known as *VAG-Zentrum*. From here it is a straight run down the west side of Besançonallee to the terminus at Munzinger Strasse. The spacious facilities here include Park & Ride, toilets, kiosk and a double-track loop. Also in evidence is the first section of track for the proposed extension to St Georgen, two kilometres further south. Four of the bus routes which terminate here were cut back from Bissierstrasse when the extension opened.

Route 5 is operated by double-ended GT8/Z type cars 241-66.

Route 6: (Yellow)
Zähringen – Rieselfeld

The first phase of route 6 was completed on 13 September 1997, when the segregated right-of-way to the new suburb at Rieselfeld began operating. The route is currently served by diverting alternate cars from route 5 at the Opfinger Strasse junction, but longer term, the route will provide a dedicated service to the city via Carl-Kistner-Strasse and Johanneskirche.

Shortly after leaving the Am Lindenwäldle stop, the tracks for route 5 swing away to the left as we continue on to the junction at Besançonallee, which we cross under traffic light priority. Construction of low rise accommodation is well advanced with many apartment blocks already occupied, although much of the area still

Two GT8/Z cars, 241 and 250, are pictured at the Bollenstaudenstrasse terminus of the Rieselfeld route on the day after its opening. Beyond lie open pastures and the Kaiserstuhl mountain.

(collection Kaufhold)

resembles a moonscape as it is prepared for construction.

Newly planted trees border the grass-covered tracks, and two intermediate stops are passed on the way to the terminus. This rather isolated spot is located at the western extremity of the site and affords a pleasant view of pastures and the distant hills. A double-track reversing loop is provided and passenger facilities include shelters and low-height platforms.

Route 6 is operated by double-ended GT8/Z cars 241-66. When the section between Am Lindenwäldle and Johanneskirche opens, it will be diverted along Opfinger Strasse and Carl-Kistner-Strasse. The proposed extension to Umkirch is unlikely to materialise for several years.

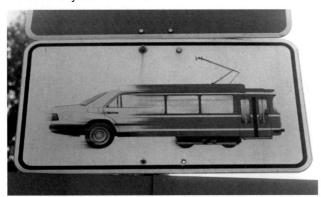

With the advent of the Stadtbahn, the VAG produced this eye-catching sign for its Park & Ride locations. Its design was based on the then new 'Auto-Bahn' theme. (author)

Operating Schedules

General

The first trams leave their depots shortly before 05.00 on Mondays to Fridays and the last cars return shortly before 02.00. A comprehensive tram and bus timetable is available free of charge and contains information on tickets and tariffs covering the whole *Regio-Verkehrs-Verbund* Freiburg area.

The availability of an enlarged tram fleet, allowed a revised timetable with shorter headways to be introduced on 10 October 1994. The following schedules were operated during the 1996/7 winter period.

Route 1

A 4-minute headway operates during the morning rush-hour (07.00 - 08.30). It is extended to 6-minutes throughout the day until 16.00, then 5-minutes through the evening rush-hour until 19.00. It then increases to 15-minutes during late evening and to 30-minutes after 23.00.

The first car enters service at 04.57 and the last car returns to the depot at 01.15.

20 trams are required to operate the peak-hour service between 07.00 and 08.30. This number reduces to 13 during the hours 08.30 to 18.30.

Route 4

A 6-minute headway is operated in the morning peak-hour, increasing to 10-minutes during the rest of the day until 19.00. It then increases to 15-minutes until 21.00, then 30-minutes until close of service.

The first car enters service at 05.00 and the last car runs in at 01.12.

9 trams are required to operate the peak-hour service between 07.00 and 08.30, reducing to 7 during the hours 08.30 to 18.30.

Routes 5 and 6

For scheduling purposes, these routes are operated as a single route between Zähringen and the Opfinger Strasse junction, where they effectively become two branches.

A 10-minute headway operates on each route in the morning rush-hour, increasing to 12-minutes through the rest of the day until 18.00, when it reduces again to 10-minutes. At 20.00 it becomes every 30 minutes and at 21.00 lengthens further to 60-minutes.

The first car enters service at 04.53 and the last car returns to the depot at 01.14.

13 trams are required to operate these services between 07.00 and 18.30.

Driver allocation

All drivers, male and female, employed by the VAG are required to be able to drive trams and buses of every type, on every route. They do not know on what mode of vehicle or which route they will be driving until they arrive at the depot for duty. This gives complete flexibility when organising the daily driving rosters.

Facts and figures

The 1995 VAG annual report confirmed that, nationwide, the number of passengers using public transport increased between 0.5 and 1%. By contrast, the number of passengers carried on Freiburg trams increased from 60.2 million in 1994 to 65.9 million in 1995, a rise of 9.5%. The major factors influencing this large increase were: the reliability, efficiency and comfort of the services, the introduction of low-floor trams, and the flexible and attractively priced ticketing structure, more restrictions on inner city parking, and the national drive for a cleaner environment.

The number of season tickets sold has seen a steady increase, year on year. In 1995, 86.5% of journeys were made using season tickets, the highest proportion for any undertaking in Germany.

A route by route analysis of VAG tram and bus passengers also revealed some interesting statistics. Tram route 1, for example, carried 35% of the overall total of passengers using VAG services. This was quite an achievement if one considers that the tram system, which comprised three routes totalling 23.1 km in length, was dwarfed by the 170 km covered by the 18 bus routes. When combined with the figures for routes 4 (11.7%) and 5 (22.3%), the total number of journeys made using the trams was 69%. The average length of a passenger journey was 3.4 km, taking an average 11.7 minutes to complete. With 62% of the permanent way segregated from vehicular traffic, high average speeds are maintained.

Recent surveys indicate that the number of cars entering the city has fallen by 4000 per day, and that 3000 fewer motorists are using the roads of the two surrounding *Landkreisen*; proof indeed that an affordable reliable and efficient public transport service does offer an acceptable alternative to the motor car.

10. Current rolling stock

Tramcar classification

With the advent of articulated tramcars, a classification system was introduced to identify the different types, usually in terms of the number of axles. In tramway parlance, the German for 'articulated motor car' is *Gelenk Triebwagen*. The system takes the letters **G** and **T** and adds the number of axles for the type of car. An 8-axle articulated car with chopper control for example, is classified as type GT8/C.

Suffixes are added to identify special features and year of entering service. These are contained in the table below:

GT *Gelenk Triebwagen*
- articulated motor car

8 *8-achsig*
- 8-axle

C *Choppertechnik*
- Chopper control

D *Drehstromtechnik*
- polyphase ac technology

M *Meterspur*
- metre gauge

N *Niederflurbauweise*
- low floor construction

Z *Zweirichtungsbetrieb*
- double-ended

93 *Im 93 in Dienst gestellt*
- entered service in 1993

This chapter gives an historical and technical summary of the rolling stock currently in service in Freiburg.

Type GT8/71: 201-204

Four 8-axle, single-ended, one-man operated, double-articulated cars were ordered by Freiburg in February 1970, as replacements for some of the 2-axle *Verbandstyp* cars, and to evaluate their capability to form the backbone of a modernised public transport system in the city. Built by Duewag of Düsseldorf and numbered 201-4, their design was based on the series of Mannheim 6-axle cars numbered 451-70.

Because of their innovative features, they were classified sub-type "Freiburg". The most prominent of these was the relocation of the second and third bogies from directly below the articulation units, as was then the standard practice, to a position under each end of an extended centre body section. The articulation units were attached to the ends of the centre section and the front and rear body sections suspended from these. This arrangement reduced the amount of body overhang on corners, allowing 8-axle cars to be operated in Freiburg.

Built of lightweight steel and with an interior floor height of 910 mm, they can carry a maximum of 294 passengers, an increase of around 70 over the standard Duewag product of the period, 89 of them on two-and-one seating and all within a 2.2-metre-wide body. At 32.846 metres, they were then the longest 8-axle articulated trams in Europe.

First generation GT8 car 203 was fitted with both a conventional controller and an automatic electronic control system, with power collected via a single-arm pantograph when it was delivered in 1971. After a year of successful running the conventional equipment was removed and electronic equipment fitted to cars 201/2/4. The cars in this batch can be distinguished by their round, centrally-located headlights. Schwarzwaldstrasse, 8/94. (author)

Second generation GT8/C car 207 dates from 1981 and differs from the 1971 batch in that it is 10 cms wider, has square headlights, a single-arm pantograph and fully automatic electronic control equipment. Schwarzwaldstrasse, 8/94. (author)

Designed for passenger flow, access is via five sets of double-width doors, the door at the front being reserved for passengers wishing to purchase their tickets from the driver. They open on the push of a button and close under the control of relays, worked by sensors under the lower steps. These prevent the doors from closing until three seconds after the last passenger has boarded or alighted.

A second major change concerned the motors. At the time of their construction it was the convention to fit single, longitudinal motors, rated at 110-120-kW, to the front and rear trucks, leaving the two inner, unpowered trucks to support the articulation units. To avoid undue stress on these units, and to provide adequate power for quick acceleration, 95-kW Brown-Boveri motors were fitted to all four bogies, giving a top speed of 70 km/h.

The electrical equipment was supplied by AEG and was similar to that fitted to the GT4 cars: conventional controllers with 18 power and 18 braking notches. Car 203 was in addition, equipped with a Geamatic automatic electronic control system from AEG, an unusual arrangement of a production car being fitted with both types of controller. A simple switch allowed the driver to change from one controller to the other. After a year of satisfactory running, cars 201/2/4 were fitted with Geamatic equipment and the conventional controllers removed from all four cars. An auxiliary controller is fitted at the rear of the vehicle for reversing the car.

Painted in the standard cream and green livery, car 201 arrived on 25 October 1971 and entered service on route 4 on 11 November. When the *Stadtbahn* opened in 1983, they were allocated to route 1 and received the red and white livery and dual headlight clusters during overhaul in the late 1980s. To celebrate 25 years service, car 201 was taken on a tour of the system by members of the FFSeV on 15 December 1996.

However, the non-availability of spares for the Geamatic equipment has required replacement parts to be handmade, a time-consuming and costly process, which has placed the long-term future of these four cars in jeopardy. The in service dates for these cars are shown below:

201	11.11.71	**203**	11.12.71
202	30.11.71	**204**	14.01.72

Type GT8/C/81: 205-214

A further ten GT8 type cars were ordered from Duewag in 1979 for operation on the *Stadtbahn*. Numbered in the series 205-14, the first car (205) arrived in July 1981 and was put to work on route 4, Littenweiler - Hornusstrasse, while construction of the *Stadtbahn* progressed.

Using similar construction techniques to those used on the first batch, these cars introduced the current, attractive red and white livery. At 2.3 metres, they were slightly wider than the first series, allowing passenger capacity to be increased to 315, 91 of whom could be seated. Ten seats were later removed to provide more space for standing passengers during rush-hours.

The windows are of rubber-mounted, tinted safety glass with opening sections at the top, additional ventilation being provided by two rows of roof mounted fans. A 50-mm layer of glass wool, supplemented by a 3-mm layer of noise absorbing material between the inner side walls and outer body panels, maintains low noise level and good thermal insulation.

A partially-enclosed driving cab contains an ergonomically designed control console. An auxiliary controller is fitted at the rear of the vehicle for reversing the car. Other changes include twin headlights, and Brown-Boveri automatic thyristor chopper control equipment.

Third generation GT8/N car 225 on grass-covered right-of-way near Landwasser, 8/94. Its low-floor centre section enabled the mobility impaired and parents with young children to become regular users of the trams for the first time. The word "Niederflur" emblazened on the dash indicates to waiting passengers that the car has a low floor. Note that this batch of cars are fitted with older style four-arm type pantographs as these were found to wear better. (author)

Each Duewag bogie is powered by a 150-kW motor driving both axles. At 32.845 metres, they were then the longest and also the most powerful 8-axle trams in Europe. The in service dates for these cars are listed below:

205	09.07.81	210	21.10.81
206	27.07.81	211	29.10.81
207	10.08.81	212	08.12.81
208	24.08.81	213	03.02.82
209	01.10.81	214	31.03.82

Type GT8/N/90: 221-231

In 1988, a third batch of eleven GT8 cars was ordered from Duewag, to cater for the continued increase in passenger loadings and to replace the ex-Stuttgart cars. Painted red and white and numbered 221-31, the first car arrived in June 1990 and all were in service by January 1991.

The design specification for the front and rear sections was similar to the previous batch, but the centre section contained a low floor extending over 9% of the total floor area. At 270 mm above railhead level, this was the lowest floor then achieved in a production tramcar. The improved accessibility proved very popular with shoppers, the mobility-impaired and mothers with children, some of whom had previously been unable to use the trams.

With an unladen weight of 38.5 tonnes, the cars are 32.846 metres long, 2.3 metres wide and provide accommodation for 84 seated and 230 standing passengers.

Equipped with the latest, state-of-the-art thyristor chopper control equipment from ABB, the cars are mounted on four identical bogies, each fitted with a single 150-kW motor. In keeping with previous Freiburg practice, both inner trucks are mounted under the ends

of the centre body section, and an auxiliary controller is fitted in the rear of the vehicle for reversing the car.

Car 221 began trial running and clearance tests on 20 July 1990, and was joined by sister car 222 in early August. They entered service on route 1 on 17 August. Cars 221-31 were the last "standard" type, high-floor GT8 tramcars to be built by Duewag, to date. The in service dates for these cars are shown in the table:

221	20.07.90	227	26.10.90
222	10.08.90	228	15.11.90
223	01.09.90	229	05.12.90
224	12.09.90	230	20.12.90
225	20.09.90	231	22.01.91
226	15.10.90		

Type GT8/D-MN-Z/93: 241-266

In January 1991 the VAG placed an order with Duewag and ABB Henschel of Mannheim, for sixteen double-articulated, low-floor cars for operation on *Stadtbahn* route 5. Designed by Duewag to a specification unique to Freiburg, these cars are 33.09 metres long and incorporate a full-width, low-floor extending through 48% of the total floor area.

Mounted on four low-height bogies, traction is provided by 8 x 80-kW, compact, water-cooled, ac polyphase motors, each driving a dedicated axle via a cardan shaft. Much of the ancillary equipment for the motors, brakes, doors, lights, etc., is located in containers on the roof.

Passenger access is via one of four sets of double doors with a step height of 290 mm. A fifth set of doors at the front is for use by passengers buying tickets from the driver. The total capacity is 326 passengers, 84 of whom can be seated. Most of the area around the doorways is devoid of seating to provide easy access for the

(left) Passengers alight from the front steps of second generation GT8/C car 208 while the driver waits patiently in his cab. Its oblong headlights are spaced farther apart and an extra 10 cms in width provides space for 21 more passengers than on the first batch. (right) On the other side of the road, passengers board third generation GT8/N car 224. Windscreen wipers were fitted to the rear of the single-ended cars to enable them to be safely driven in reverse when running-in during wet weather-most commonly between Runz mattenweg and Betriebshof West. Bertoldsbrunnen, 7/97. *(author)*

mobility-impaired and people with push chairs and shopping trolleys. Tinted safety glass windows are fitted throughout.

The fully-enclosed driving cabs are air conditioned and contain a small bench seat behind that of the driver, for use by driving instructors. A joystick type controller, operating through automatic thyristor control and anti-slip processors, provides fast and smooth acceleration and braking.

Car 241 was delivered to Komturstrasse depot on 23 September 1993. Following unloading, it was driven to Urachstrasse works for inspection and acceptance checks, and test running commenced between Wonnhalde and Wiesenweg on 4 October.

It was painted all-over blue with yellow doors depicting the cabins on the *Schauinslandbahn*. By contrast, 242, which arrived on 3 November, was painted red and adorned with slogans advancing the benefits of travelling by tram compared to the private car. Car 243 was delivered in late November in the standard red and white livery. Car 241 was the first of the series to enter service on route 4 on 3 December 1993.

Twelve cars were available for the opening of the extension to Munzinger Strasse on 26 March 1994. The

official first cars were given names during the opening ceremonies in recognition of the occasion; 243 – *"Zähringen"*, 246 – *"Weingarten"* and 247 – *"St Georgen"*.

Following the decision to replace all the GT4s in the spring of 1992, the order for GT8/Z cars was increased to 26. Numbered 257-66 and identical to the first batch their delivery commenced in July 1994 and was completed by December. The GT8/Z cars operate predominantly on routes 4, 5 and 6, and several are in all-over advertising liveries. The in service dates for these cars are listed in the table:

241	24.11.93	254	20.04.94
242	09.12.93	255	03.05.94
243	21.12.93	256	10.06.94
244	19.01.94	257	04.08.94
245	22.01.94	258	24.08.94
246	04.02.94	259	09.09.94
247	10.02.94	260	22.09.94
248	13.02.94	261	30.09.94
249	02.03.94	262	13.10.94
250	12.03.94	263	20.10.94
251	18.03.94	264	16.11.94
252	25.03.94	265	25.11.94
253	05.04.94	266	16.01.95

These two views show the distinctive lines of the GT8/Z cars which are unique to Freiburg. Powered by eight, compact 80-kW ac motors, and mounted on four small bogies, they have an extraordinary low-floor height. Car 255 (above) is seen at Runzmattenweg in September 1996, while brand new sister car 257 (below) gleams as it stands in Betriebshof West, 8/94. (author)

Works cars

Most of the early works cars were purpose-built for their intended tasks, street-washing, snow-clearing, rail-grinding, etc. As time progressed however, it became prudent to adapt withdrawn passenger vehicles for these roles, and over the years, several such conversions were carried out.

Despite the various fleet number allocations over the years, many works and advertising cars retained their final passenger car numbers. Some early works cars were subsequently saved for preservation as described in the "Museum car" section.

The number of works cars has steadily dwindled over the years and at the time of writing consists of a few converted *Verbandstyp* motor cars numbered 401/2/4/5/6, a Schöma diesel-powered permanent way car numbered 407" and miscellaneous trailers. Most are painted in a bright orange livery which was introduced in 1970.

Three other *Verbandstyp* cars were converted for use as depot shunters; 403 (ex-71), 405 (ex-69) and 407

Driver training car (Fahrschulwagen) 401 was converted from motor car 65 in 1970. Repainted red and white in 1994, it has dual controls and instructor seats at both ends and twin conductor desks in the centre for training staff manning the museum cars. It wi *become a dual-purpose vehicle when the overhead line inspection equipment is transferred from car 402 in 1998. Behind it is the diesel powered general purpose vehicle 407". Betriebshof West, 8/94.* *(author*

Overhead line car (Messwagen) 402, converted from motor car 70 in 1970, poses with single-axle snowploughs 422 and 423, durir a test run near Wonnhalde. Following the removal of its inspection equipment, it is anticipated that car 402 will join the museum fleet 1998. *(collection Kaufhold/Hettinge*

(ex-73), but these were withdrawn in 1989, 1981 and 1977 respectively. 403 and 407 were scrapped, and 405 obtained by the SMS museum in Schönau.

In September 1994, *"Sputnik"* 103 was panelled over and repainted green to become an advertising car and renumbered 100, its original number. A selection of current works cars are shown on these two pages:

Cars 404 and 406 are depot shunters (Rangierwagen) and were converted from motor cars 64 and 72 in 1972. Here we see the latter pulling Verbandstyp trailer 236 out of Halle II at Komturstrasse depot during the final week of trailer operation, 26/6/81.

(collection Kaufhold/Hettinger)

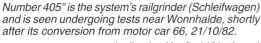
Number 405" is the system's railgrinder (Schleifwagen) and is seen undergoing tests near Wonnhalde, shortly after its conversion from motor car 66, 21/10/82.

(collection Kaufhold/Hettinger)

Having performed their last passenger duties in December 1993, "Sputniks" 102 and 103 were reassigned–the former as a museum car but unfortunately scrapped in 1996–the latter as advertising car 100. They are seen in Betriebshof Nord with some of the museum cars, 22/4/95.

(collection Kaufhold)

The table below lists the works cars currently operated by the VAG and their in-service dates:

No.	Built by	Date	Purpose	Notes
100	Rastatt	09/94	Advertising car	"Sputnik", ex-100, ex-103'''
401	Rastatt	07/70	Driver trainer	ex-Motor car 65
402	Rastatt	05/70	Overhead inspection	ex-Motor car 70
404	Rastatt	01/72	Depot shunter	ex-Motor car 64
405"	Rastatt	10/82	Railgrinder	ex-Motor car 66
406	Rastatt	10/71	Depot shunter	ex-Motor car 72
407"	Schöma	10/82	Permanent way	Diesel powered
209"	Tramway dept.	01/28	Truck	First numbered in 1962: 416 in 1971
210"	Tramway dept.	01/28	Truck	First numbered in 1962: 417 in 1971
211"	Tramway dept.	12/53	Truck	First numbered in 1962
411	Diema	09/82	Ballast truck	
412	Diema	09/82	Ballast truck	

Museum cars located in Freiburg

The creation of a representative collection of historical Freiburg trams has only recently been taken seriously. With a little luck and a great deal of determination by local enthusiast Herr Hettinger, two trams were kept when similar cars were being scrapped in the 1960s. These formed the basis of a museum fleet which has recently expanded following the formation of the *Freunde der Freiburger Strassenbahn e.V* (FFSeV)

museum society on 2 December 1994. Two preservation candidates, *Verbandstyp* motor car 74 and *"Sputnik"* 102 were unfortunately scrapped in 1996, but more recently, the VAG has taken a greater interest in the preservation of its tramcars, through the availability of its workshop facilities and the retention of a representative selection of vehicles, GT4 car 109 and the release of works car 402 being a prime examples. The current list of preserved cars is shown in the following table:

No.	Built by	Type	Date	Notes
2	HAWA	2xZR	12/61	VAG museum motor car, not operational
38"	MAN	2xZR	12/71	FFSeV museum motor car. Ex-DSM
45	MAN	2xZR	12/71	FFSeV museum motor car, under restoration. Ex-DSM
56	Rastatt	4xZR	07/68	VAG museum motor car
74	Rastatt	2xZR	01/78	VAG partywagen. Scrapped 1996
102"	Rastatt	4xGelER	01/94	VAG museum motor car. Scrapped 1996
109""	Esslingen	4xGelZR	08/97	VAG museum motor car
121"	Rastatt	4xGelZR	05/95	VAG partywagen
135	Rastatt	2xZR	07/81	VAG museum trailer car, not operational, ex-235
142	Rastatt	2xZR	07/81	VAG museum trailer car, ex-242
414	Schörling	2xZR	07/82	VAG museum works car, not operational

FFSeV = Freunde der Freiburger Strassenbahn e.V.

(above, left) Car 2 is the oldest surviving Freiburg tramcar. A 2-axle motor car dating from 1901, it was used as an advertising car from 1951 until 1961, when it was sold to Herr Hettinger. It was later repurchased by the VAG and last ran under its own power during the opening of the Stadtbahn in 1983. (above, right) Schörling railgrinder 414 (ex-203), which dates from 1930, is the only purpose-built works car so far preserved. It became a museum car in 1982 after eleven years in store and was captured at Komturstrasse depot hauling motor car 2 out of Halle II, on 3/8/81. *(collection Kaufhold/Hettinger)*

The second preserved car is maximum-traction motor car 56. which, following its withdrawal in July 1968, was bought for preservation by Herr Hettinger. Built in 1927 by Rastatt, it is now owned by the VAG, and is currently used for private-hire and special occasions. is seen here outside Hauptbahnhof on the last day of service along Bismarckallee, 27/9/86. *(collection Kaufhold)*

In 1992, 2-axle motor cars 38" and 45 were retrieved from the Deutsches Strassenbahn Museum (DSM) in Wehmingen in poor condition after twenty years open to the elements. The FFSeV museum society began the refurbishment of car 45 in 1995 and hope to return it to fully working condition in time for the centenary celebrations in 2001. It is seen here at Betriebshof West during the "Tages der offenen Tür" in the summer of 1995. (collection Kaufhold)

In 1994, GT4 car 109"" was being prepared for sale to Halberstadt when it was realised that it was the first GT4 car in Freiburg. The VAG decided to retain it as a possible museum car and sent sister car 115 instead. In 1997, the VAG confirmed that 109"" would join the museum fleet and that it will eventually bear its original cream livery and number, 103. It is seen here running past Komturstrasse depot while working a route 3 circular service, 7/93. (author)

The future of GT4 car 121 was secured in 1995 when it was converted for use as a Partywagen. Painted in its brewery-sponsored dark blue livery, it has seating for 31 people, a bistro, disco and dance area, and is seen here at Landwasser during an FFSeV tour of the system, 20/4/97. (collection Kaufhold)

The following Freiburg cars went to established museums and other interested bodies following their withdrawal:

4"/43	DSM in Wehmingen, Hannover	227/32/8/40	SMS museum in Schönau. Scrapped in 1995
2	Fahrzeug Museum at Marxzell (MM) near Karlsruhe	237	DMS museum, Wehmingen
0	Kindergarten in Landwasser - scrapped	236/9	Private collectors in Waltershofen and Grunern respectively. 239 scrapped in 1983.
)	Trucks to the DSM in Wehmingen, Hannover	243	Kindergarten at Waisenhaus, Günterstal, scrapped 1988
4"/9	Strassenbahn Museum Schönau (SMS), near Heidelberg. Scrapped in 1995.		

Information on the FFSeV museum society's activities and a regular newssheet, can be obtained from:
ndreas Kaufhold, Freunde der Freiburger Strassenbahn e.V., Jahnstrasse 34, D-79117 Freiburg im Breisgau.
ermany.

11. Depots

At the time of writing there are three operational depots *(Betriebshöfe);* two are for trams only and one for both trams and buses.

Betriebshof Süd (Urachstrasse)

The oldest of the three depots, the first section was completed in 1901. At that time it had five, 62-metre storage tracks with a capacity for 35 two-axle tramcars. Workshop facilities were provided for repair and maintenance and an extensive administration building was constructed alongside the depot with offices, toilets and changing facilities.

By 1907, the expanding fleet caused several cars to be stored outside in the depot forecourt. Organising trams for the daily schedule became a nightmare. In May of that year, the council approved construction of a 6-track extension, to be built in the same style. When completed in 1908, 77, two-axle tramcars could be accommodated under cover.

As the system continued to expand, a second depot was opened at Komturstrasse in 1928 and some of the operating fleet transferred there. After the last war, all tram services were operated from Komturstrasse, and the role of Urachstrasse changed to that of a central works. It is currently responsible for the repair, maintenance and overhaul of the trams, and upkeep of the permanent way, but will become redundant once these tasks are transferred to Betriebshof West. When this happens, Urachstrasse will probably be handed over to a city utility as it is subject to a preservation order.

Betriebshof Nord (Komturstrasse)

The silver jubilee report of 1926 identified the need for a new depot to relieve the cramped conditions at Urachstrasse, which would become intolerable following the arrival of the maximum-traction cars.

A piece of land was purchased at Komturstrasse in the north of the city and ambitious plans prepared for a 15-track depot, workshop and administration block. The financial constraints in force at that time however, caused a scaling down of the project and a 5-track depot to house 30 cars was all that could be afforded. Construction began in 1926 and the new depot (known internally as *Halle I*) was opened on 8 May 1928. A 3-track open yard for works cars, and an extension to the depot *(Halle II)* was added in 1935.

With the easing of restrictions on materials and finance after the second world war, preparations were made for the acquisition of new trams and expansion of Komturstrasse. Work on digging the foundations for a second depot *(Halle III)* began in November 1948 and it was opened on 15 April 1950. It was 90 metres long and contained 6 storage tracks, enough to house 48 *Verbandstyp* cars. An extension containing two tracks was added later. Trams can access the depot from either end.

The arrival of the 8-axle cars introduced several problems. Firstly, they could not all be housed under cover, so some were stored overnight in the works yard. Secondly, as they were single-ended, a series of awkward shunting manoeuvres, much of it in reverse, were required to store them in *Halle I*.

A fine view of Urachstrasse Btf, circa 1927, with motor cars 37, 45, 16, 26, 24, 52, 15, 30, 2 and 3 ready to take up their duties, durin the period when it was operating at maximum capacity. Apart from the trams, the scene has changed very little in the intervening yea and the building, which has a preservation order on it, would make an ideal home for the museum cars when the VAG decides relinquish it.
(E.Baumgartne

Betriebshof West (Besançonallee)

Komturstrasse depot forecourt was also home to the bus fleet for several years, but as the number of buses increased through the 'sixties, congestion became a serious problem. In 1967 it was decided to build a new depot on a virgin site which had plenty of space to expand.

A 10 hectare (100 000 m²) plot of land was purchased in Besançonallee, in Auf der Haid in the south west, and digging of the foundations commenced at the end of the year. When it became operational in 1970, accommodation was provided for 80 buses together with all the maintenance, repair and testing equipment required for a large fleet. As it was anticipated that a third tram depot would be needed, maintenance facilities for the trams were incorporated from the outset.

Following the opening of the *Stadtbahn* and the acquisition of more trams in the 1980s, the decision was taken to transfer some of them to Besançonallee. Two adjoining depots (*Wagenhallen I* and *II*) were built, each containing four storage tracks, enough to accommodate a total of 36 eight-axle cars. A broad range of equipment for the maintenance, repair, overhaul and repainting of the trams is housed in a spacious workshop complex. Accommodation for the administration is provided in a new two-storey office block, built just inside the entrance and overlooking an extensive forecourt.

The depot was connected to the system as construction of the *Stadtbahn* progressed towards Auf Der Haid. Betriebshof West became an operational tram depot with the opening of route 5 on 26 March 1994.

Besançonallee. A greater proportion of the tram fleet is now housed in one of the two large "Wagenhallen" in this extensive tram and bus complex. Vehicle maintenance and overhauls are carried out in a modern, surgically clean environment, a major reason for the immaculate condition of the cars. The last classical Duewag-built GT8 tramcar with high-floor sections, number 231, awaits a duty as an extra on route 1.
(author)

Wagenhalle III at Komturstrasse is the setting for this 1971 lineup of trams, which includes 2-axle museum motor car number 2, 2-axle works car 42, Verbandstyp motor car 73 and GT4 car 106.
(collection Kaufhold/Hettinger)

12. Tickets and fares

The "Umwelt Karte"

In 1984, three types of ride-at-will tickets, valid for 24 hours (DM 5.0), 48 hours (DM 8.0) and 72 hours (DM 11.0), offered unlimited travel on Freiburg's tram and bus routes. For regular travellers weekly season tickets valid for 6 (DM 12) or 7 (DM 13) days were also available. On 1 October that year, a new environmental fare structure was introduced inspired by the system used in nearby Basel. It was the first of its kind in Germany and proved so successful, that other transport undertakings introduced versions of their own. The new system was called the "Auto-Bahn Karte", a play on words to encourage motorists to transfer from their cars to public transport. With the growing concern over pollution, it was later renamed "Umwelt Karte" (Environmental ticket).

A "gentlemen's" agreement between Freiburg and Basel, which allowed Umwelt Karten issued by one system to be valid on the other, was in force for several years.

For a cost of DM 5.0, the purchase of an Umwelt Karte entitled motorists to park their car at one of the park-and-ride facilities and enjoy up to 24 hours unlimited travel on all VAG services. With a validity for two adults and four children, demand soon exceeded expectations. In 1985, for example, over 253 000 Umwelt Karten were sold, this figure increasing to more than 400 000 in 1990. Sixty percent of all journeys were undertaken with this ticket with record numbers of people regularly using public transport for the first time. In 1993, the number of passengers travelling on VAG services exceeded 60 million, and 647 000 Umwelt Karten were sold.

On 1 January 1996, the Regio-Verkehrs-Verbund Freiburg (RVF) was formed, incorporating the services operated by the VAG, 16 local bus companies and the Deutsche Bundesbahn rail lines within the Landkreisen of Freiburg, Emmendingen and Breisgau-Hochschwarzwald. The VAG's environmental ticket was expanded to cover the whole region and renamed "Regio-Karte" (Regional Ticket), and is valid on all public transport services within the area. Changes in the political administration of the German Railways (now Deutsche Bundesbahn AG) might lead to changes in some of the facilities available.

The "Regio-Tarife"

Various classes of the Regio-Karte are available within the Regio-Tarife (fare tariff), providing access to 79 bus services, 4 tram routes and 8 sections of Deutsche Bahn AG railway lines, operating over 2900 route kilometres. The area is organised into three zones, with the four tram routes running within the central zone (A) only.

On 29 September 1996, the following Regio-Tarife were put into operation:

TICKET	1 ZONE	2 ZONES	3 ZONES	SPECIAL
Einzelfahrschein (Single)	DM	DM	DM	DM
Adult	3.20	5.50	7.80	
Child	1.60	2.80	3.90	
Punkte-Karte (Multi-ride)				
Adult	2.80 (x7)	4.80 (x 12)	6.40 (x 16)	
Child	1.20 (x3)	2.40 (x 6)	3.20 (x 8)	
Regio24 (24-hour)				
1 adult (+ 4)	7.50		15.00	
2 adults (+ 4)	10.00		20.00	
Regio-Monatskarten (Monthly)				
Everybody			64.00	
Student (under 26 - in education)		47.00		
Junior (under 26 - not in education)		57.00		
Regio-Jahreskarte (Annual)				
Everybody			640.00	
Schauinslandbahn				
Adult return				18.00
Partywagen				
Hourly rate				140.00

Notes:
- The number of equivalent rides in the Punkte-Karte category are shown in brackets (e.g. x12).
- The Regio24-hour ticket is valid for one or two adults, and up to four children under the age of 15.
- Tickets can be purchased from the VAG information centre "PlusPunkt" at 3 Salzstrasse, the VAG kiosk on Bahnhofsbrücke, DB AG and SWEG ticket machines, the various bus companies, certain retail outlets and from drivers.
- Dogs can travel at the child rate.
- The Schauinslandbahn currently operates from 09.30 - 17.00 from 1 October to 30 April, and from 09.00 - 18.00 between 1 May to 30 September. It is not included in the Regio-Tariffe.
- The minimum hire period for the Partywagen is 2 hours, so the minimum fare is DM 280.

13. Further expansion

Objectives

The *Stadtbahn* provides the primary framework for public transport services in the city. The ability of the tram to transport people quickly and efficiently, in a clean and comfortable environment, and at an affordable price, are the fundamental reasons for the high and rising ridership figures.

During the last few years, a programme of limiting on-street parking to residents only was implemented, 30 km/h speed limits introduced and further restrictions on the motor car are envisaged, including barring access to many roads currently used for through traffic. The cycle path network has been progressively upgraded and extended to its current 410 km.

So what prospects does the future hold for the *Stadtbahn*? On 26 April 1994, Freiburg Council and the VAG published a series of detailed proposals, covering the expansion and modernisation of the system over the next twenty years or so, based on the plans outlined in the *General Verkehrs Koncept*. The ultimate goal is to give 90% of the population access to public transport within 300 metres of their homes.

Each item was given a priority and placed in one of four categories: short term new; short term upgrade; long term new; and long term upgrade. The proposals for the *Stadtbahn* outlined below are not necessarily in the order in which they will materialise, as this will depend on circumstances prevailing at the time.

Short Term (new construction)

- *1.24-km* **branch** on segregated right-of-way from Opfinger Strasse to a new suburb at Rieselfeld, via Rieselfeldallee. Opened as route 6 on 13 September 1997.

- *3.5-km* **new route** on *trambaan* from Johannes-kirche, Basler Strasse, Carl-Kistner-Strasse, and Opfinger Strasse, replacing bus routes 11 and 12. Work will start in 1999 and the line will open in two stages–to Haslach in 2001; the remainder in 2006.

Short term (upgrade)

- *1.5-km* **trambaan** in Hansjakobstrasse, route 1. Planned for 1998.
- *0.3-km* **trambaan** in Schwarzwaldstrasse, route 1. Planned for 1998.
- **Modernisation programme** for tram stops. Currently in progress.

Long term (new construction)

- *1.6-km* **extension** from Lassbergstrasse to Littenweiler Bahnhof, and on tracks laid alongside the DBAG Freiburg – Titisee Neustadt railway line, to Kappler Strasse. A start on this extension is dependent on progress with construction of a new section of the B31 relief road, which will cut through this area.
- *1.8-km* **extension** of route 5 from Zähringen to Gundelfingen Süd via Zähringer Strasse and Gundelfinger Strasse.
- *6.0-km* **new route** from Basler Strasse to Merzhausen and St Georgen, via Merzhauser Strasse and Wiesentalstrasse, replacing bus route 10.
- *1.5-km* **extension** from Munzinger Strasse to St Georgen Friedhof.
- *2.1-km* **new trambaan** from Stadtgarten via Siegesdenkmal, Kronenstrasse and Rotteckring for

During the weekend of the opening of the Rieselfeld extension, museum cars 56 and 142, the latter performing its first duty since being restored, gave citizens free rides between Rieselfeld and Hornusstrasse. The set is pictured at the new terminus stop, 14/09/97
(collection Kaufhold)

the Merzhausen route, and to provide a relief and diversionary route for Kaiser-Joseph-Strasse.

- *2.3-km* **new route** from Siegesdenkmal to *Flugplatz* (airport) via Fehrenbachallee and Breisacher Strasse. This will probably be brought forward as a new *Messe* and shopping centre will open near the airport in 1999.
- *3.5-km* **extension** to Hochdorf from *Flugplatz*.
- *4.0-km* **extension** from Rieselfeld to Umkirch.
- *1.5-km* **extension** from Gundelfingen Süd to Gundelfingen Bahnhof.

Long term (upgrade)

- ***Trambaan*** in Habsburgerstrasse.
- ***Trambaan*** in Komturstrasse.
- ***Trambaan*** in southern section of Kaiser-Joseph-Strasse.

Priority was given to the Rieselfeld extension as construction of accommodation for 12 000 people was scheduled to begin in 1995. Work on the line commenced in March 1996 and it was opened on 13 September 1997, as described in chapter 8. By the end of 1997, approximately 2000 people were living in Rieselfeld, requiring a 10-minute headway to be operated. This will gradually reduce to 6-minutes as the number of inhabitants reaches 10 000 at the turn of the millennium.

Work was completed in 1996, on installing a new layout at the Littenweiler terminus of route 1, the initial phase of *trambaan* construction in Hansjakobstrasse. This should be completed in 1998 when construction is scheduled to commence on the route from Johanneskirche to Opfinger Strasse.

New Trams

In August 1997, the VAG placed an order with Duewag/Siemens for nine, double-ended, 42-metre long, seven-section "*Combino*" trams, with capacity for 340 passengers. Five cars are due for delivery in 1999 and four in 2000, and an option was signed for a further eight cars in 2001. *Combino* is the name given to the new family of modular light rail vehicles introduced by the Transportation Systems Group of Siemens AG. Cars can be purchased in configurations of 3, 4, 5, 6, or 7 modules.

The modules are constructed of aluminium extruded sections with aluminium sidewalls, comprising standardised corner, door and window posts, bolted to a welded underframe. The roof of the smaller modules comprises an aluminium and plastic sandwich, which is glued onto the side and end members. A terminal box, ventilator and cable ducting are mounted in a container on top. One module is additionally fitted with the pantograph container, housing the main circuit breaker and 600/750 volt dc distribution. The end modules are constructed from fibreglass reinforced-plastic and contain the destination display and heating, ventilation and air-conditioning equipment for the driver's cab. A pre-assembled and pre-tested electronic cabinet and instrument panel is installed in each end module.

The 100% low-floor requires that the car is mounted on four Duewag low-height bogies. Motive power is provided by 8 x 100-kW three-phase ac motors, each of which transfers torque through bevel gears to two wheels on one side of its bogie.

The current intention is to introduce the *Combino* cars on route 1, and transfer the high-floor GT8/C cars to route 6 as this has higher platforms at the tram stops.

The VAG has ordered nine Combino articulated cars from Siemens AG for delivery in 1999/2000, with an option for a further eight i the following year. Based on the prototype car above, the freiburg version will be 42 metres long, have seven sections and be abl to carry up to 340 people on the heavily utilised route 1   *(Siemens AG*

These three photographs depict some of the locations from which the new extensions will be built.
(top) GT8/Z car 253 at the Zähringen terminus. The extension here will fork right by the building in the centre-background and head north in two stages to Gundelfingen Bahnhof. (centre) The Am Lindenwäldle junction with GT8/Z car 266 on route 5. Currently, the tracks here turn left into Binzengrün, but as the construction of new routes gains momentum, route 6 will continue straight on and along Opfinger Strasse towards Johanneskirche. (lower) GT8/Z car 252 lays-over at the Munzinger Strasse terminus. The section of stub-end track was laid during construction of the line in anticipation of its extension to St Georgen. (author)

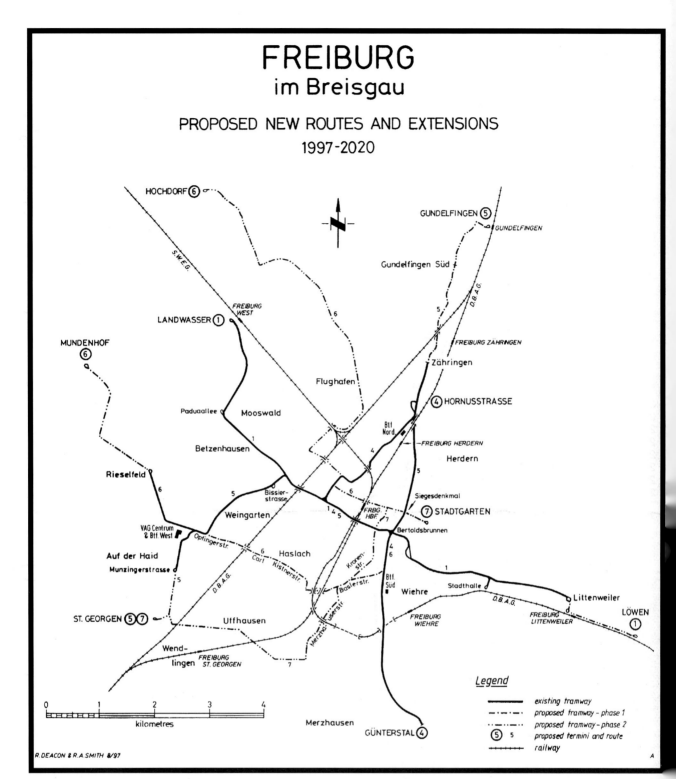

FREIBURG
im Breisgau

PROPOSED NEW ROUTES AND EXTENSIONS
1997-2020

Legend

▬▬▬	existing tramway
–·–·–	proposed tramway - phase 1
·····–··	proposed tramway - phase 2
⑤ 5	proposed termini and route
+++++	railway

R. DEACON & R.A. SMITH 8/97

Conclusion

For a city the size of Freiburg, the *Stadtbahn* will play an increasingly dominant role, as the programme of replacing bus routes, or changing their role to that of feeders to the trams, is implemented. Over the next fifteen to twenty years, approximately 30 km of new tram routes and extensions should become a reality, more than doubling the size of the current system.

The VAG's policy of introducing an advanced and attractively-priced ticketing system, combined with modern, high capacity, low-floor tramcars, operating at high frequencies on segregated rights-of-way, backed up by a comprehensive network of subsidiary bus services, has invoked a mood of change in attitudes to public transport in the city. An increasing number of people are leaving their cars at home to make use of these excellent services, as the ridership figures in chapter 9 clearly demonstrate. This has already led to a 50 percent reduction in traffic accidents and a 60 percent reduction in their severity.

The evolution of the *Stadtbahn* in Freiburg shows just how possible it is to implement a modern public transport system in a modestly-sized city, and at the same time, enhance the quality of life for its inhabitants. The tramcar of today is once again proving that is the vehicle to fulfil the traffic requirements of tomorrow. The future bodes well for the city and the trams of Freiburg.

14. Withdrawn trams

2-axle Passenger Motor Cars

No.	Built by	Renumbered No.	Date	New Role	Withdrawn Date	Notes
Cars 1-27, type 2xZR, entered service Oct 1901						
1	Hawa				11/44	Destroyed in bombing
2	Hawa	W2	10/51	Advertising car	12/61	VAG preserved car
3	Hawa	111	09/53	Trailer	01/60	
4	Hawa	108	12/53	Trailer	01/60	
5	Hawa				05/50	
6	Hawa	110	07/53	Trailer	01/60	Advertising car 11/50-07/53
7	Hawa				11/44	Destroyed in bombing
8	Hawa				03/49	
9	Hawa				11/44	Destroyed in bombing
10	Hawa	105	12/54	Trailer	01/60	
11	Hawa	W11	03/51	Advertising car	05/62	
12	Hawa	211	01/52	Works car	12/61	
13	Hawa	207	01/52	Works car	12/61	
14	Hawa	208	01/52	Works car	05/62	
15	Hawa	209	01/52	Works car	05/62	
16	Hawa				04/50	
17	Hawa	212	01/52	Works car	12/61	
18	Hawa	107	08/54	Trailer	01/60	
19	Hawa				06/42	
20	Hawa	W20	09/50	Works car	10/51	
21	Hawa	210	01/52	Works car	05/62	
22	Hawa				11/44	Destroyed in bombing
23	Hawa				11/47	
24	Hawa				07/51	
25	Hawa	106	10/54	Trailer	01/60	
26	Hawa	109	10/53	Trailer	01/60	
27	Hawa	201"	10/49	Works car	12/61	
Cars 28"-30", type 2xZR, entered service in Jun/Jul 1907						
28"	Rastatt				01/59	
29"	Rastatt				10/59	
30"	Rastatt				05/55	
Cars 31'''-40", type 2xZR, entered service Mar/Jun 1909						
31'''	MAN					
32"	MAN				10/16	Destroyed in train collision
33"	MAN					
34"	MAN	W34	01/62	Shunter	11/69	DMS Wehmingen
35"	MAN					
36"	MAN					
37"	MAN					
38"	MAN	W38	04/60	Brake test car	10/71	FFSeV museum car
39"	MAN					
40"	MAN	32'''	1917		07/56	
Cars 41-47, type 2xZR, entered service Oct 1901						
41	MAN	W41	01/62	Stores car	10/71	
42	MAN	W42	09/61	Shunter	10/71	Farhzeug Museum, Marxzell
43	MAN	W43	01/62	Stores car	11/69	DMS Wehmingen
44	MAN				11/44	Destroyed in bombing
45	MAN	W45	12/60	Shunter	10/71	FFSeV museum car
46	MAN	W46	09/61	Stores car	11/66	
47	MAN	40'''	1920		11/66	Stores car W40 from 10/60
Cars 47"-56, type 4xZR, entered service Jun 1927						
47"	Fuchs				11/67	
48	Fuchs				12/61	
49	Fuchs				07/68	
50	Fuchs				06/68	Kindergarten, Landwasser
51	Fuchs				11/67	
52	Fuchs				10/65	
53	Rastatt				11/44	Destroyed in bombing
54	Rastatt				11/67	
55	Rastatt				08/61	
56	Rastatt				07/68	VAG museum car

2-axle Passenger Motor Cars

No.	Built by	Renumbered No.	Date	New Role	Withdrawn Date	Notes
Cars 57-61, type 4xZR, entered service August 1929						
57	Rastatt				12/61	
58	Rastatt				07/68	
59	Rastatt				12/61	
60	Rastatt	W60	1968	Driver trainer	08/70	Trucks to DSM
61	Rastatt	53"	1951		11/67	
Cars 61"-74, type 2xZR (*Verbandstyp*), entered service Apr-Jul 1951, Dec 1953-Feb 1954						
61"	Rastatt				06/79	SMS, Schönau
62	Rastatt				10/73	
63	Rastatt				01/74	
64	Rastatt	404	01/72	Depot shunter		
65	Rastatt	401	07/70	Driver trainer		
66	Rastatt	405"	10/82	Railgrinder		
67	Rastatt				06/73	
68	Rastatt				06/73	
69	Rastatt	405	10/71	Depot shunter	07/81	
70	Rastatt	402	10/70	Overhead line car		
71	Rastatt	403	05/70	Depot shunter	03/91	
72	Rastatt	406	10/71	Depot shunter		
73	Rastatt	407	01/71	Depot shunter	10/77	
74	Rastatt		01/78	VAG Partywagen	03/96	

A fine shot of maximum-traction car 60, turning short at Lorettostrasse for a run to Zähringen, 10/6/66. Following withdrawal from passenger service in 1968, and two years as a driver-trainer, its trucks were dispatched to the DSM museum and its body scrapped. (J. Thompson)

Verbandstyp motor car 61 was the last of its type in passenger service and is seen passing Hauptbahnhof, 25/02/79. After a period in store, it was sold to the SMS museum near Heidelberg where it was scrapped in 1995. (collection Kaufhold)

4-axle Passenger Motor Cars

No.	Built by	Renumbered No.	Date	Withdrawn Date	Notes
Cars 100-102", type 4xGelER ("Sputnik"), entered service Oct/Nov 1959					
100	Rastatt	103'''	09/67	01/94	To works fleet as advertising car 100
101"	Rastatt			12/93	
102"	Rastatt			01/94	
Cars 103"-113''', type 4xGelZR (GT4), entered service Jul-Jan 1962 / Jan/Feb 1966					
103"	Esslingen	109''''	09/67	1997	VAG museum car
104"	Esslingen			11/97	To Halberstadt as HVG 166
105'''	Esslingen			07/94	To Halberstadt as HVG 161
106'''	Esslingen			12/94	To Halberstadt as HVG 164
107'''	Esslingen				In store
108'''	Esslingen			12/94	To Halberstadt as HVG 165
109'''	Esslingen	114'''	09/67	05/94	To Nordhausen as VSR 94
110'''	Esslingen			05/94	To Nordhausen as VSR 91
111'''	Esslingen			06/94	To Nordhausen as VSR 92
112'''	Esslingen			01/94	To Nordhausen as VSR 93
113'''	Esslingen			07/94	To Halberstadt as HVG 162
Cars 115'''-122", type 4xGelZR (GT4), entered service Dec 1967-Jan 1968 / Dec 1968-Jan 1969					
115'''	Rastatt			08/94	To Halberstadt as HVG163
116'''	Rastatt			10/97	To Brandenburg as BBRv 116
117'''	Rastatt			10/97	To Brandenburg as BBRv 117
118"	Rastatt			09/97	To Brandenburg as BBRv 118
119"	Rastatt			08/93	To Nordhausen for spares
120'''	Rastatt			01/94	To Nordhausen as VSR 120
121"	Rastatt			05/95	VAG partywagen
122"	Rastatt			07/94	To Nordhausen as VSR 122
Cars 151-160, type 4xGelER (GT4), ex-Stuttgart, built 1964, entered service Aug 1985-Dec 1988					
151	Esslingen	ex-SSB 700		07/90	To Halle as HAVAG 851
152	Esslingen	ex-SSB 704		07/90	To Halle as HAVAG 852
153	Esslingen	ex-SSB 687		06/90	To Halle as HAVAG 853
154	Esslingen	ex-SSB 693		07/90	To Halle as HAVAG 854
155	Esslingen	ex-SSB 702		07/90	To Halle as HAVAG 855
156	Esslingen	ex-SSB 703		07/90	To Halle as HAVAG 856
157	Esslingen	ex-SSB 705		07/90	To Halle as HAVAG 857
158	Esslingen	ex-SSB 706		09/88	Scrapped
159	Esslingen	ex-SSB 730		07/90	To Halle as HAVAG 859
160	Esslingen	ex-SSB 696		07/90	To Halle as HAVAG 858

Ex-Stuttgart cars 158 and 152 wait to depart from Landwasser on a peak-hour extra on route 1, 4/87. Car 158 suffered a serious technical defect and was scrapped in the summer of the following year. (collection Kaufhold/Hettinger)

2-axle Passenger Trailers

No.	Built by	Renumbered No.	Renumbered Date	Renumbered No.	Renumbered Date	Withdrawn Date	Notes
Cars 28-31, type 2xZR, entered service Oct 1901							
28	HAWA	31"	1907	101	01/09		
29	HAWA	35	1907	102	01/09		Open-sided
30	HAWA	36	1907	103	01/09		Open-sided
31	HAWA	37	1907	104	01/09		Open-sided
Cars 32-34, type 2xZR, entered service Oct 1903							
32	Rastatt			105	03/09		
33	Rastatt			106	03/09		
34	Rastatt			107	03/09		
Cars 38-40, type 2xZR, entered service Mar 1907							
38	Rastatt			108	03/09		
39	Rastatt			109	03/09		
40	Rastatt			110	03/09		

Passenger trailer cars built in or renumbered after 1909

No.	Built by	Renumbered No.	Renumbered Date	Renumbered No.	Renumbered Date	Withdrawn Date	Notes
101	HAWA					03/54	
102	HAWA			W102	12/17	07/40	Goods wagon
103	HAWA			W103	12/17	07/40	Goods wagon
104	HAWA			W104	12/17	07/40	Goods wagon
105	Rastatt			113"	11/51	07/60	
106	Rastatt			112"	11/51	07/60	
107	Rastatt					11/44	Destroyed in bombing
108	Rastatt	121	12/49	221	09/67	06/69	Rebodied by Rathgeber
109	Rastatt	125	08/50	225	09/67	06/69	Rebodied by Rathgeber
110	Rastatt					11/44	Destroyed in bombing

Cars 111-120, type 2xZR, entered service Mar-Jul 1909

No.	Built by	Renumbered No.	Renumbered Date	Renumbered No.	Renumbered Date	Withdrawn Date	Notes
111	Rastatt	116"	03/50	216	09/67	11/68	Rebodied by Rathgeber
112	Rastatt	114"	1951			05/62	
113	Rastatt	115"	1950			05/62	
114	Rastatt	117"	10/49	217	09/67	01/72	Rebodied by Rathgeber
115	Rastatt	120"	02/50	220	09/67	11/68	Rebodied by Rathgeber
116	Rastatt	124	07/49	224	09/67	01/72	Rebodied by Rathgeber
117	Rastatt	122	12/49	222	09/67	06/69	Rebodied by Rathgeber
118	Rastatt	118	10/49	218	09/67	11/68	Rebodied by Rathgeber
119	Rastatt	119	02/49	219	09/67	01/72	Rebodied by Rathgeber
120	Rastatt	123	02/50	223	09/67	01/72	Rebodied by Rathgeber

Passenger trailer cars converted from motor cars

New No.	Old No.	In service Date	Withdrawn Date
105"	10	12/54	02/60
106"	25	10/54	02/60
107"	18	08/54	02/60
108"	4	12/53	02/60
109"	26	10/53	02/60
110"	6	07/53	02/60
111"	3	09/53	02/60

Two of the seven motor cars converted for use as trailers in 1953/4, cars 106" an 107" (ex-18 and 25 respectively), were captured whilst laying over outside Urach strasse Btf.
(collection Kaufhold/Hettinge

2-axle Passenger *Verbandstyp* Trailers

No.	Built by	Renumbered No.	Date	Withdrawn Date	Notes
Cars 126-134, type 2xZR, entered service May-Sep 1950 / Aug 1951					
126	Rathgeber	226	09/67	09/79	
127	Rathgeber	227	09/67	07/81	SMS, Schönau
128	Rathgeber	228	09/67	09/79	
129	Rathgeber	229	09/67	09/77	
130	Rathgeber	230	09/67	09/79	
131	Rathgeber	231	09/67	09/77	
132	Rathgeber	232	09/67	07/81	SMS, Schönau
133	Rathgeber	233	09/67	09/79	
134	Rathgeber	234	09/67	07/81	
Cars 135-143, type 2xZR, entered service Nov 1952 / Dec 1953 / Feb 1954					
135	Rastatt	235	09/67	07/81	VAG museum car
136	Rastatt	236	09/67	07/81	Waltershofen
137	Rastatt	237	09/67	07/81	DSM Wehmingen
138	Rastatt	238	09/67	07/81	SMS, Schönau
139	Rastatt	239	09/67	07/81	Grunern
140	Rastatt	240	09/67	07/81	SMS, Schönau
141	Rastatt	241	09/67	06/81	
142	Rastatt	242	09/67	07/81	VAG museum car
143	Rastatt	243	09/67	07/81	Günterstal

This 1954 scene shows 1903-built trailer 112" at the Herdern terminus of route 5. The car changed very little throughout its working life. (W.Stock)

Verbandstyp trailer 241 waits to be towed into Komturstrasse depot in the late evening sunshine. (collection Kaufhold/Hettinger)

73

Works motor cars

No.	Built by	In service as works car	Purpose	Withdrawn Date	Notes
201	J. Hellmers	07/08	Water car	01/49	MEG, Lahr
201"	HAWA	10/49	General duties	12/61	ex-Motor car 27
202	J. Hellmers	02/12	Water car	12/61	
203	Schörling	03/30	Railgrinder	07/82	Renumbered 414 in 1971
206	AEG	12/27	Electric trolley	10/61	Not railborne
207	HAWA	01/52	Advertising car	12/61	ex-Motor car 13
208	HAWA	01/52	General duties	05/62	ex-Motor car 14
209	HAWA	01/52	General duties	05/62	ex-Motor car 15
210	HAWA	01/52	General duties	05/62	ex-Motor car 21
211	HAWA	01/52	General duties	12/61	ex-Motor car 12
212	HAWA	01/52	General duties	12/61	ex-Motor car 17
403	Rastatt	05/70	Depot shunter	09/89	ex-Motor car 71
405	Rastatt	10/71	Depot shunter	07/81	ex-Motor car 69. SMS in 1981
407	Rastatt	01/71	Depot shunter	10/77	ex-Motor car 73

Works trailer cars

No.	Built by	In service as works car	Purpose	Withdrawn Date	Notes
204	J. Hellmers	08/01	Brine car	10/68	Also used as overhead line car
205	Tramway dept.	01/09	Brine car	10/71	Renumbered 415 in 1971
206"	O & K	01/08	Truck	01/72	First numbered in 1962
207"	O & K	01/08	Truck	01/72	First numbered in 1962
208"	Tramway dept.	01/28	Truck	01/72	First numbered in 1962
413	Cemafer	12/82	Rail-carrier	05/90	Two section
422	Tramway dept.	02/69	Snow plough	01/77	Single-axle
423	Tramway dept.	02/69	Snow plough	01/77	Single-axle

Works cars retaining their original numbers

No.	Built by	In service as works car	Purpose	Withdrawn Date	Notes
2	HAWA	10/51	Advertising car	12/61	VAG museum car
3	HAWA	04/51	General duties	09/53	Converted to trailer 111"
4	HAWA	06/51	General duties	12/53	Converted to trailer 108"
6	HAWA	11/50	Advertising car	07/53	Converted to trailer 110"
11	HAWA	10/51	Advertising car	05/62	
20	HAWA	09/50	General duties	10/51	
25	HAWA	09/50	General duties	10/51	Converted to trailer 106"
26	HAWA	01/52		10/53	Converted to trailer 109"
34"	MAN	01/62	Depot shunter	12/71	DMS, Wehmingen
38"	MAN	04/60	Brake-test car	03/72	FFSeV museum car
40'''	MAN	10/60	Stores car	03/67	
41	MAN	01/62	Stores car	10/71	
42	MAN	09/61	Depot shunter	12/71	Fahrzeug museum, Marxzell
43	MAN	01/62	Stores car		
45	MAN	12/60	Depot shunter	03/72	FFSeV museum car
46	MAN	09/61	Stores car	12/66	
60	Rastatt	1968	Driver trainer	08/70	Trucks to DSM
102-4	HAWA	12/17	Goods wagons	07/40	Former open-sided trailers

Notes on the re-use of fleet numbers

Throughtout the text and in the fleet lists, we have used the convention that when a car number was re-used it is distinguished by a double apostrophe as a suffix. Motor car 28 of 1907 for example, is shown as 28" as this number was originally applied to a 1901 trailer. Any further re-use is shown by the addition of an extra apostrophe for each re-use. Only in this way can a number be associated with the correct car.

Technical specifications – motor cars

Fleet Nos.	Builder	Year Built	Length metres	Weight tonnes	Seats	Capacity	Motors	Type	Notes
1-27	HAWA	1901	7.53	9.00	16	30	2x9kW	2xZR	
28-30	Raststt	1903	9.43	13.00	20	44	2x25kW	2xZR	a
31-40	MAN	1909	9.43	13.50	20	44	2x25kW	2xZR	b,c
41-47	MAN	1914	9.70	13.00	20	44	2x25kW	2xZR	c
47-52	Fuchs	1927	11.10	16.50	26	50	2x37kW	4xZR	d
53-56	Rastatt	1927	11.10	16.50	26	50	2x37kW	4xZR	
57-61	Rastatt	1929	11.10	16.50	26	50	2x37kW	4xZR	d
61-74	Rastatt	1951/3	10.50	13.20	22	70	2x60kW	2xZR	
100-102	Rastatt	1959	17.43	19.00	39	160	2x100kW	4xGelER	
103-113	Esslingen	1962/6	18.00	20.50	40	171	2x100kW	4xGelZR	
115-122	Rastatt	1967/8	18.00	20.50	40	171	2x100kW	4xGelZR	
151-160	Esslingen	1964	18.00	19.50	48	177	2x100kW	4xGelER	
201-204	Duewag	1971/2	32.85	36.00	89	294	4x95kW	8xGelER	e
205-214	Duewag	1981/2	32.85	38.00	91	316	4x150kW	8xGelER	
221-231	Duewag	1990/1	32.85	39.57	84	313	4x150kW	8xGelER	f
241-266	Duewag	1993/4	33.09	38.50	84	326	8x80kW	8xGelZR	g

Technical specifications – trailer cars

Fleet Nos.	Builder	Year Built	Length metres	Weight tonnes	Seats	Capacity	Motors	Type	Notes
28	HAWA	1901	7.52	6.50	16	46		2xZR	h
29-31	HAWA	1901	7.53	9.00	18	46		2xZR	
32-34	Rastatt	1903	8.02	6.50	16	30		2xZR	h
38-40	Rastatt	1907	8.02	7.50	16	30		2xZR	h,j
111-120	Rastatt	1909	9.19	7.50	16	54		2xZR	h,i,j
116-125	Rathgeber	1949/50	9.45	8.00	22	70		2xZR	
126-134	Rathgeber	1950/1	10.43	7.50	26	70		2xZR	
135-143	Rastatt	1952/3	10.50	7.50	22	70		2xZR	
105-111	HAWA	1953/4	7.53	9.00	16	30		2xZR	k

Notes:

a Platforms lengthened in Urachstrasse depot before entering service. Radial trucks replaced in 1925.

b Single-axle radial trucks replaced between 1936-40.

c 34/6/8/41/3 fitted with 37-kW motors removed from maximum-traction cars between 1951-4.

d 47"/9-52/8/60/53" fitted with 60-kW motors between 1953-60.

e 203" fitted with conventional and automatic control systems for first year of service.

f Low-floor centre section, 9% of total floor area.

g Low-floor for 48% of total floor area.

h Fitted with bow-type current collectors for heating and light.

i 114/5 received fully enclosed platforms in 1936/8.

j 38/9/111/4/5/6/7/8/9/20 rebodied by Rathgeber in 1949/50.

k Converted from 1901 motor cars in 1953/4.

n extensive permanent way yard was once located in Kaiserstuhlstrasse. Behind railgrinder 414, withdrawn motor cars 42, 45, 38", *nd 34" await their departure to various museums, while depot shunter 403 is sandwiched between open wagons 208", 210" and 209", *nd maximum-traction car 56 shelters under a tarpaulin in the background, 1/12/71.* (collection Kaufhold/Hettinger)

Light Rail Transit Association

The LRTA is a UK-based international organisation campaigning for the
construction, retention and development of modern tramways and light rail.
Membership is open to everyone; all members receive the monthly magazine
Tramways & Urban Transit
by post.
Membership details from
The Membership Secretary, LRTA,
23 Shrublands Close, Chigwell, Essex IG7 5EA
Annual subscriptions normally run to the end of the calendar year, with
different rates for the UK, mainland Europe and outside Europe. Full details
are obtainable from the address above.
There is also a quarterly (mainly UK) historical magazine
Tramway Review,
available to members at a reduced subscription.
Ask for details

LRTA Publications

This book was published by LTRA PUBLICATIONS.
If you liked it, you will find that we publish (sometimes jointly) books on
international trams (some available currently and others in preparation include national handbooks on Germany, the former Soviet Union, Portugal,
Switzerland and Austria).
We also publish a series of regional handbooks British tramways, and a
limited number of hardback histories, mainly of the London area.

LRTA members often have the opportunity to buy newly-published LRTA
books (and sometimes also others) at discounted prices.

Further details from:

LRTA Membership Secretary
23 Shrublands Close, Chigwell, Essex IG7 5EA

A book price list is available

Dedication

The idea for this book hit me like a bolt of lightning when a close family member asked me why there are so few books about Mrs. Claus. I had to tell the truth! Thanks, Denise!

And to all my BFFs out there—you WILL make it to the other side of menopause— and I'll be waiting for you with a glass of wine!

Audience: Women of a certain age—and their friends
Illustrations by Luis Peres
Cover and Layout by Praise Saflor

For information: www.bestfairybooks.com
ISBN: 979-8-9868490-7-2 ...Hardcover $17.95
ISBN: 979-8-9868490-8-9 ...Paperback $12.95

Publisher's Cataloging-in-Publication data

Names: Hinman, Bobbie, author. | Peres, Luis, illustrator.
Title: Mrs. Claus has menopause / by Bobbie Hinman; illustrated by Luis Peres.
Description: St. Cloud, FL: Best Fairy Books, 2023.
Identifiers: LCCN: xxxxxxxxxx | ISBN: ISBN: 979-8-9868490-7-2 | 979-8-9868490-8-9 Subjects: LCSH Menopause--Humor. | Middle-aged women--Humor. | Santa Claus--Fiction. | Christmas stories. | Humorous stories. | BISAC HUMOR / General | HUMOR / Topic / Health & Aging | FICTION / Humorous / General | FICTION / Holidays | FICTION / Women Classification: LCC PN6231.M453 H56 2023 | DDC 612.6/65—dc23

MRS. CLAUS
HAS MENOPAUSE

Written by
Bobbie Hinman

Illustrated by
Luis Peres

Mrs. Claus has menopause.
The deer all have the flu.
But gifts must be delivered...
WTF will Santa do?

Right now she's sitting in the fridge
with chocolate on her face,
and in her hand a glass of wine,
while feeling no disgrace.

So Santa calls the doctor,
and demands to find the cause.
"Oh Doc, I think she's flipping out!"
Doc says, "Nope! Menopause!"

"Doc's using that word, *menopause*.
I see it starts with *men*.
Does that imply that it's MY fault?
Crap! There she goes again."

She screeches, "Men are stupid!
They just care about themselves!
But *you*, my dear, are even worse...
Your friends are deer and elves!"

"Help, Doc! She cries at everything!
It's ramping up my fears."
Doc says to just be patient...
says it only lasts 10 years!

So Santa tries to suck it up,
pretending hard to care.

One minute she feels happy,
but that doesn't last too long.
Her mood swings up, then crashes down.
"What the fudge did I do wrong?"

She's opened all the windows,
and still swears she's freaking hot.
Poor Santa's wearing 16 coats,
and sleeping on a cot.

"What ARE these *flashes* she describes?
The situation's dire!
Last night the wife was so damn hot,
she set my beard on fire!"

"Do I look fat in this red cape?
she asks, to my dismay...
then steadily gives me THE LOOK."

"Her sweats at night are killing me,
so bye-bye, nighttime cuddles.
Each time she tries to cool herself,
the snowmen turn to puddles."

"That's it," says Santa, "I must get
my gift drop under way."
But wifey can't remember
where she parked the gosh darn sleigh!

With so much work ahead this night,
poor Santa's running late.
"Just one more thing," yells wifey...
"Do you think I'm gaining weight?"

The deer are feeling better,
but since ladies think alike...
The girl elves, sad for Mrs. Claus,
are marching and on strike.

When Santa finally leaves the house,
he hears her from within...

"What's next?" she shrieks, "I'm sprouting little hairs upon my chin!"

As Santa leaps into his sleigh,
he's finally feeling free.
"Bye bye, my menopausal wife!
Enjoy the Christmas tree!"

"Whatever!" says the missus,
as she hides her sheer delight.
"Let's strip down to our party clothes,
and whoop it up all night!"

ABOUT THE AUTHOR
BOBBIE HINMAN

Bobbie Hinman is an editor and multi-award-winning children's book author. Her goal has always been to make children smile, but the time has come to share a bit of humor with her BFFs... and all the women of the world.

Visit Bobbie's website: www.bestfairybooks.com

ABOUT THE ILLUSTRATOR
LUIS PERES

Luis Peres has been professionally illustrating dreams for thirty years. In addition to children's books, Luis has created art for games, apps, prints and greeting cards. His preferred artistic style is imaginary worlds.

Visit Luis' website: icreateworlds.com

WE HOPE YOU ENJOYED THIS BOOK.

If you enjoyed this book,
please tell your friends about it.

A review on Amazon is always appreciated.
Simply scan the code, or follow the link,
and you will land on the review page. Enjoy!

www.bit.ly/mrsclause-menopause

Printed in Great Britain
by Amazon

Enjoy a comical look at Mrs. Claus
as she goes through the night sweats, mood
swings, and other issues
that women *of a certain age*
will identify with.

A perfect gift for the moody friends
on your Christmas list.

Bobbie Hinman is an editor and multi-award-winning
children's book author. Her goal has always been to make
children smile, but the time has come to share a bit of
humor with her BFFs... and all the women of the world.

Best Fairy Books
Bestfairybooks.com

ISBN 979-8-9868490-8-9

51295

9 798986 849089

MY FIRST 100 WORDS

ENGLISH | YORUBA